Contents

2 THE HUMAN BODY
4 SCIENCE
6 MEDICINE
7 OUR PLANET AND BEYOND
9 MYTHOLOGY & LEGENDS
10 WEATHER
11 CALENDAR FACTS
12 TRAVEL
14 ARCHITECTURAL LANDMARKS
15 CONSTRUCTION MATERIAL
16 LAW & ADMINISTRATION
17 WAR
19 HISTORICAL EVENTS
20 AMAZING PEOPLE

INTERESTING INVENTIONS 23
TECHNOLOGY 26
THE FIRST . . . 28
PRECIOUS STONES AND METALS 31
FAITHS & BELIEFS 32
FOOD 33
TREES AND PLANTS 36
INSECTS 37
BIRDS AND ANIMALS 38
REPTILES 43
LIFE UNDERWATER 44
BOOKS 45
MAKING MUSIC 46
GAMES & SPORTS 47

FASCINATING FACTS 49

500 Questions & Answers

Written by Peter Eldin
Edited by Joanna Davies

Packaging & Designer: Q2A Design Studio.

First published by Grandreams Books Limited 4-5 North Parade, Bath

Printed in Thailand

The Human Body

What are goose pimples?

Goose pimples are little bumps that appear on our skin when we are cold. The cold air causes muscles at the base of hairs on the skin to stiffen, resulting in these small bumps. The hairs stand up, trapping air between them and giving the body some insulation against the cold.

What makes body hair stand on end?

When you are frightened you may feel a tingling sensation down the back of your neck. This is your hair standing on end! It is caused by small muscles at the root of each hair. Although it is not very visible in humans you can see it clearly when a cat is frightened. Its hairs stand erect so the animal appears bigger to its enemies.

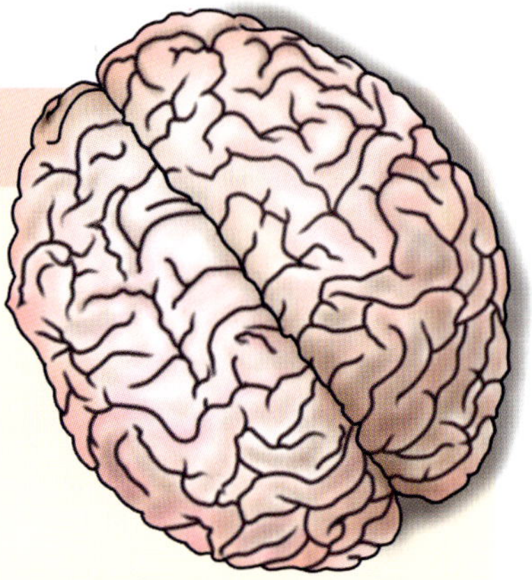

How heavy is the human brain?

For men, the average weight is just over 1.36 kilograms (3 lb). Womens' brains are about 1.25 kilograms (2 lb 12 oz).

Which is our largest muscle?

The largest muscle is the buttock muscle, which you use to lift your legs. It is called the gluteus maximus.

Which muscle has the longest name?

Just curl your upper lip and you'll be using the human muscle with the longest name: the levator labii superioris aleoquae nasi.

Why do we have eyebrows?

Although we have hair all over our bodies, it tends to grow thickest where some form of protection is needed. Both eyebrows and eyelashes are designed to protect the eyes from dust.

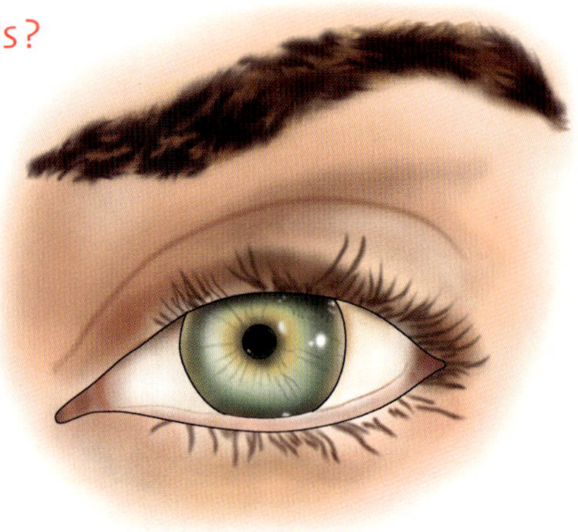

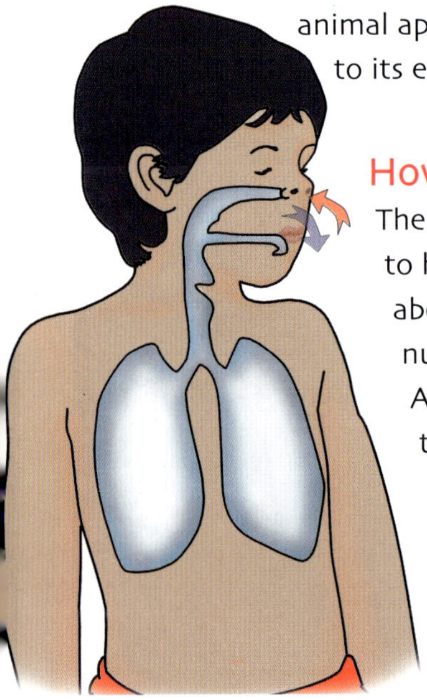

How often do we breathe?

The rate at which a person breathes varies according to his or her age. A newborn baby breathes in and out about 65 times a minute. By the age of 15, the number of breaths per minute decreases to about 20. As a person gets older, the rate decreases further. By the age of 40 he or she is breathing approximately 18 times a minute. These figures vary according to health, level of fitness and whether or not one is standing still or is active at the time.

Which is our smallest muscle?

The smallest muscle in the human body is attached to the smallest bone. Called the stapedius, it controls the stirrup bone and is only 0.127 centimetre (1/16 in) long.

How many teeth do we have?

Unfortunately, not many people have a full set of teeth. They decay or have to be taken out because we eat too many sweet things or do not look after them properly. However, a full set in an adult would consist of 32 teeth.

What causes a heart attack?

Blood is carried to the heart by the arteries. If an artery gets blocked, the blood cannot get through and the heart cannot function properly. As a result, the heart is damaged, causing a heart attack. The arteries get blocked due to a variety of health factors.

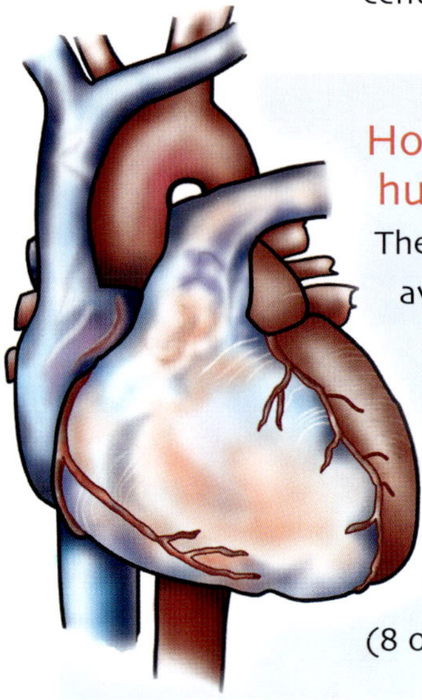

How heavy is the human heart?

The heart of an average adult man weighs about 300 grams (10 oz). The heart of an average woman is lighter and weighs around 250 grams (8 oz).

Why do skin types vary?

The colour of a person's skin depends upon the amount of melanin it contains. Melanin is a brown substance present in everyone's skin. Ultra-violet rays in sunlight cause the skin to produce more melanin and this is why people in hot climates have a darker skin than those who live in cooler areas of the world. The purpose of the melanin, which is deposited on the outer layers of the skin, is to protect the skin from the sun.

What is the purpose of a yawn?

One usually yawns when bored or tired. Yawning makes you draw in breath, filling your lungs with air. This increases the oxygen supply to the blood to help wake yourself up.

Why do people blink?

Every time we blink, normally about six times a minute, a tear is secreted by the lachrymal gland in the corner of the eye. This tear spreads over the cornea to keep the eyeball clean and moist. The amount you blink increases when wind, dust or bright light threatens to harm the eye.

Why do people get wrinkles?

As a person gets older the body fat is renewed less readily. Because of this, the skin has a smaller area to cover and so it wrinkles up.

What is a stitch?

A stitch is a pain felt on either side of the body, usually after severe exertion. It is caused when normally inactive muscles tighten and press against the nerves. In a healthy person, a stitch is nothing to worry about and soon passes.

What is a wart?

It is a growth on the skin that is caused by a virus. Although unsightly, warts are usually painless. They should only be removed by a doctor who will either freeze or burn them off with acid.

Can you get warts from toads?

Many people believe that you can get warts from toads because the toad's skin is covered with bumps. But it is just superstition - you cannot get warts from toads.

How many bones do you have?

It depends upon how old you are. Young people have more bones than adults. As a person grows up, some bones separate and increase the number, while other bones fuse to reduce the number. By the time a person reaches full adulthood, there are normally 206 bones in the body.

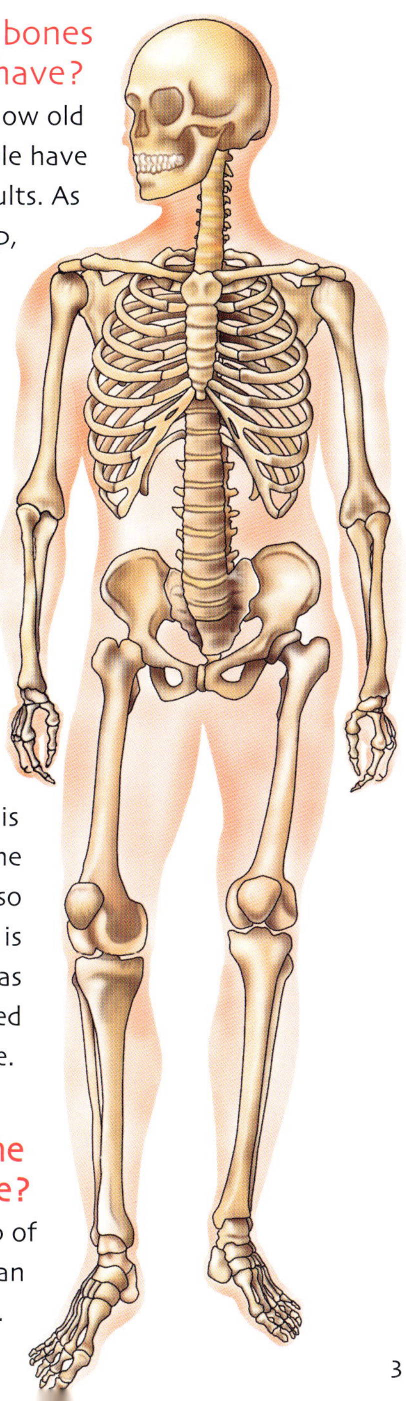

What is the shortest bone?

The shortest bone is the stirrup. It is in the inner ear. It is so called because it is the same shape as a stirrup used on a saddle.

What is the longest bone?

Well, it is not the spine for that is made up of several bones. The longest bone in the human body is the thigh bone, or femur.

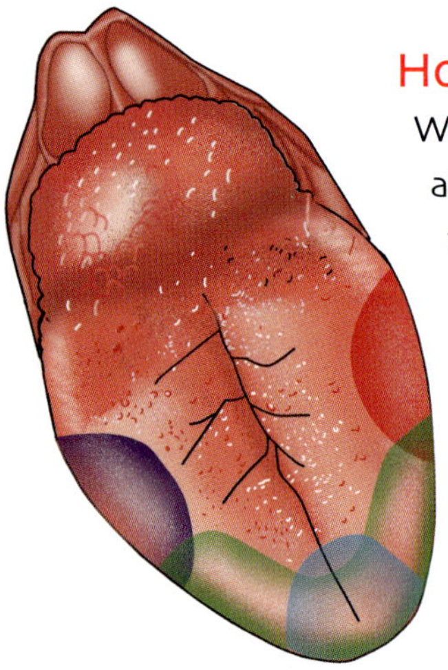

How do we taste food?

With our taste buds. The tongue is covered with about 3,000 of them. When they are stimulated, the taste buds send messages to the brain. These messages are interpreted as different tastes according to where the taste bud is located on the tongue. The tip of the tongue, for example, is particularly sensitive to salty or sweet foods; the back discerns bitter tastes; and the sides respond to anything sour. Our perception of taste is also affected by the smell, appearance and the texture of food.

What is a bruise?

Bruises are caused by the rupturing of blood vessels under the skin. Gradually, the blood decomposes and is absorbed. As this happens, the blood loses oxygen and turns blue. Later, it changes to green and yellow until it eventually disappears altogether.

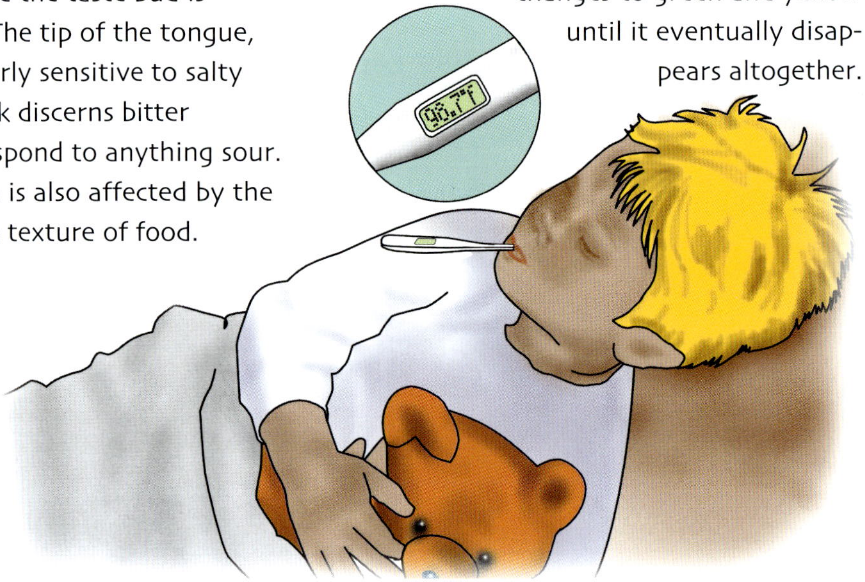

What is the normal temperature of the human body?

The average normal body temperature is 36.9˚C (98.4˚F). Body temperature is a general indication of good or bad health, which is why doctors often take patients' temperatures.

Science

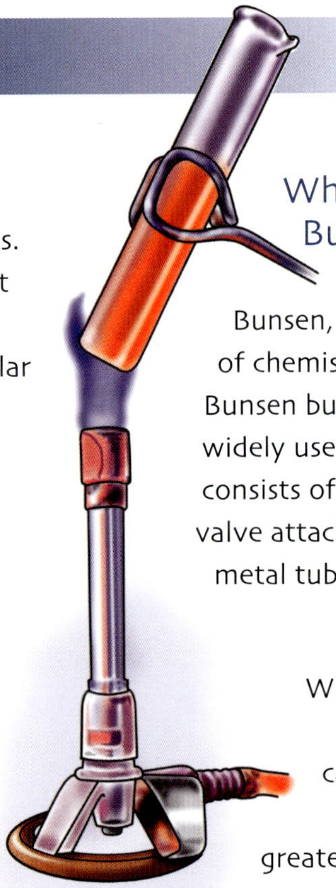

What is an element?

All matter consists of elements. An element is a substance that cannot be broken down into anything simpler. This particular definition was given by the chemist Robert Boyle in the 17th century and it still holds true today.

How many elements are there?

There are 94 natural elements: two are liquids, 11 are gases and 81 are solids.

Who invented the Bunsen burner?

Robert Wilhelm Bunsen, a German professor of chemistry, developed the Bunsen burner in 1855. It is a widely used gas burner that consists of an adjustable air valve attached to the base of a metal tube.

Which gases are found in air?

Air is a mixture of gases, the main ones being oxygen and nitrogen. There are also small amounts of carbon dioxide, argon, neon, helium, xenon and krypton.

How does a Bunsen burner work?

When oxygen is combined with gas, the gas burns with a greater heat. The Bunsen burner has a metal collar at its base which can be turned to expose holes in the main cylinder. When these holes are open, oxygen is drawn in and the flame burns with a greater intensity. Strangely, not all parts of the flame have the same temperature. The brightest part, in the middle of the flame, burns at about 300°C (527°F). The hottest part of the flame is at the top, where it is almost invisible, and has a temperature of about 1,550°C (2,822°F).

How was the sundial invented?

The sundial was probably devised by people who noticed that shadows change length and direction during the day. As a result, early man developed the shadow stick, which over a period of time was developed into the sundial.

How does a barometer work?

There are two main types of barometer - mercury and aneroid. The mercury barometer houses a glass tube containing mercury. The height of the column of mercury in the tube is controlled by air pressure on the mercury. When the atmospheric pressure falls (an indication of forthcoming wind or rain), the pressure on the mercury is decreased and some of it runs out from the base of the tube into a special container. When the pressure rises (indicating fair weather), the mercury is forced back up into the tube. In most barometers, the tube of mercury is hidden and its movements operate a dial on the front of the barometer. Aneroid barometers work on a different principle. Inside the aneroid barometer is a small metal box with a thin lid. Most of the air has been withdrawn from the box so it contains springs which prevent the box from being crushed by the air pressure. The lid of the box is moved up and down by the air pressure and this movement is monitored by a lever that makes the pointer move across the dial on the front of the barometer.

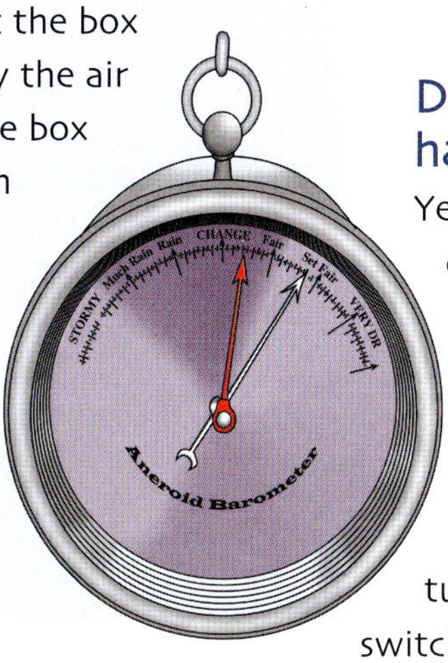

How does an aerosol work?

When it was first invented in 1942, the aerosol was called the 'bug bomb' because it contained insecticide for use by American military forces. Today, under its modern name of 'aerosol', the bug bomb has a thousand and one different uses - from making air smell fresher to cleaning ovens and from producing whipped cream to spraying on bandages. The modern aerosol is made of a tube of tin-plate or glass, at the top of which is a plastic plunger and valve. Leading from the valve is a dip tube through which the contents are propelled. With the product, there is a liquid which turns to gas at room temperature. Pressure exerted by the gas pushes the contents of the dip tube up and out through the nozzle when the plunger is pressed.

What is an Archimedean screw?

It is an ancient means of raising water from a river or ditch. It consists of a long tube with a large screw fitted inside. When one end of the screw is placed in the water and the handle is turned, water rises through the tube and comes out of the top. Although it is named after the Greek inventor Archimedes, it is quite likely that this device, or something similar, was around long before he was born.

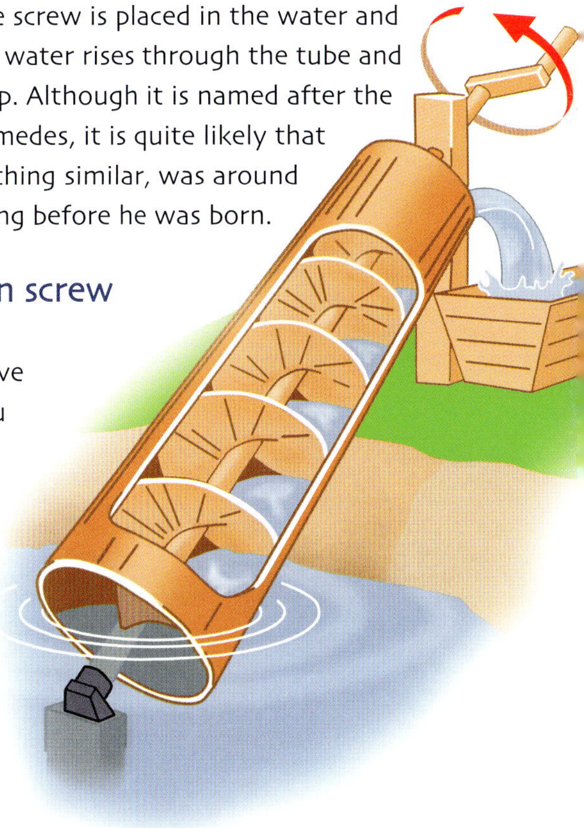

Does the Archimedean screw have other uses?

Yes, and you might even have one in your kitchen. If you look at a food mincer, you will find that it also consists of a large screw within a tube. When the handle is turned, or the electricity switched on, the food is forced along the screw and through the tube. At the front end of the mincer is a metal grill with a perforated disc attached. The food is forced through the holes in the disc and is minced.

How does a kaleidoscope work?

Inside the tube of a kaleidoscope there are two or three mirrors positioned at an angle of 60° to each other. Placed between the mirrors are pieces of coloured paper or plastic. What the viewer sees, as well as the pieces of plastic or paper, are their reflections in the mirrors. These images can form a colourful pattern which is changed by shaking the kaleidoscope or by revolving the end section of the tube.

How does a vacuum flask work?

A vacuum flask consists of a glass or metal bottle with double walls from which the air has been removed. Heat cannot travel through a vacuum but it is possible for some heat to radiate from one wall to the other. This is why the innermost wall is silvered - so that the heat is reflected back into the bottle.

What is the Beaufort scale?

Admiral Sir Francis Beaufort devised the Beaufort Scale in 1806. It is used to record wind speed. The Beaufort Scale categorises wind speed on a scale of 0 to 12, 0 being calm weather and 12 a hurricane.

Medicine

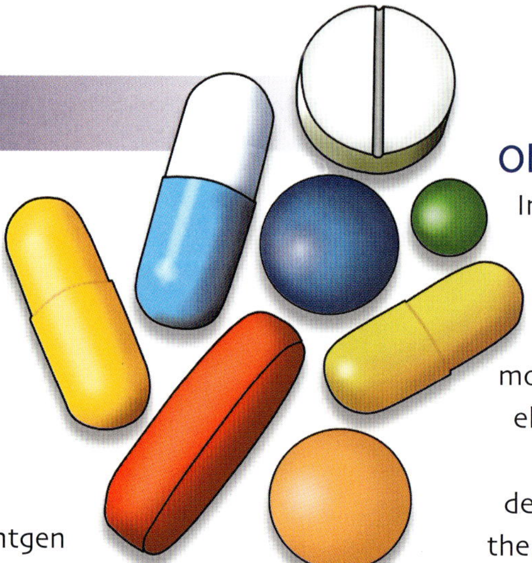

What are antibiotics?

Antibiotics are chemicals produced by a micro-organism that can stop bacteria growth or destroy other bacteria. Their development has revolutionised the treatment of disease.

When were X-rays discovered?

In 1895, the German scientist Wilhelm Van Roentgen was studying the behaviour of electricity in a vacuum tube (one end of which was coated with fluorescent salts). After one experiment, he found that a nearby photographic plate looked as if it had been exposed - even though it was covered. Van Roentgen concluded that some form of 'invisible rays' had come from the tube and affected the plate. He named them X-rays, as so little was known about them. Further research found these rays could pass through materials such as cardboard and wood, but were stopped by materials like lead and bone. The scientist quickly realised that X-rays would have great medical use and today every large hospital has an X-ray department.

Why is the village of Oberammergau famous?

In the 17th century, the village of Oberammergau in the Bavarian Alps was afflicted by the bubonic plague. As more and more people died, the elders called all the villagers to church, and they agreed to devote one year in every ten to the presentation of a play, called the Passion Play, dramatising the death and resurrection of Jesus Christ. After that promise, there were no more deaths from the plague and, with the exception of the war years, the play has been performed every ten years since 1634. The whole village takes part and people flock from all over the world to watch.

What is a stethoscope?

It is an instrument used by physicians to listen to sounds emitted from various organs, particularly the lungs.

Who invented the stethoscope?

The stethoscope was invented in 1814 by a French doctor, René Theophile Laennec. Early stethoscopes consisted of a wooden tube about 30 centimetres (12 in) long.

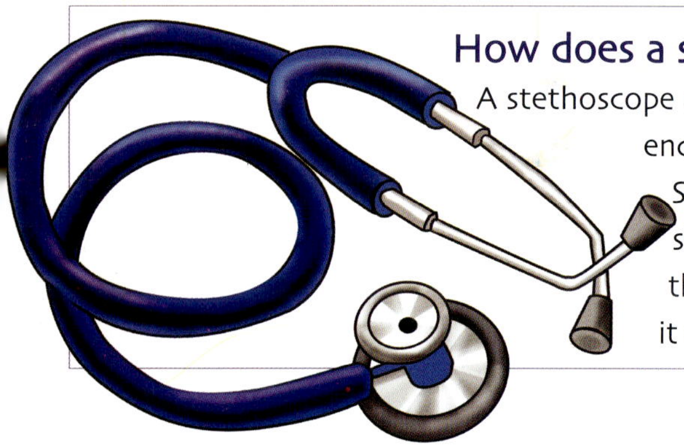

How does a stethoscope work?

A stethoscope amplifies the sound received from one end placed against the patient's body. Sound waves are reflected from side to side as they pass along the tube, thus the sound is concentrated which makes it easy for the doctor to hear.

What was the 'Black Death'?

The Black Death is a name given to the bubonic plague that spread from Asia to Europe in the 14th century. The disease was carried by fleas on infected rats which were found on ships traveling from the Far East. It is estimated the disease killed between 25 and 50 per cent of the European population.

What is a placebo?

A placebo is a harmless drug or pill. Placebos are given to people who think they are ill when really they are not. They are also used as a contr-olled substance in medical tests.

What is acupuncture?

Acupuncture is the ancient Chinese practice of curing certain ailments by pricking the skin with long needles. Very often the needles are inserted well away from the affected part of the body. This is because there are thought to be special channels, called meridians, flowing through the body and each meridian serves a particular organ.

Who invented acupuncture?

It was Emperor Fu Shi, who lived some 5,000 years ago in China. He believed everything was a balance of two forces: Yin and Yang. Fu Shi also thought the forces to be in the human body, remaining in balance unless illness struck. The purpose of acupuncture is to restore this balance.

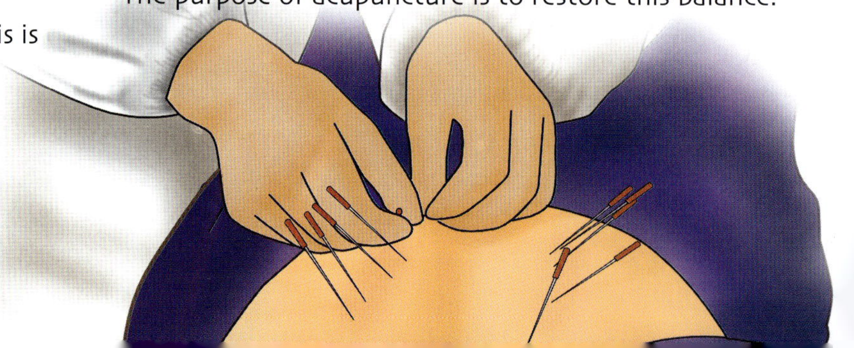

Our Planet and Beyond

What is a comet?

There are three parts to a comet: the nucleus, or head, which is made up of ice and particles of debris; the coma, gases that surround the nucleus; and the tail, which is composed of small dust-like particles and may be millions of kilometres in length. Comets travel around the sun, approaching it head first and leaving it tail first.

What is the largest meteorite ever found?

The largest known meteorite still lies where it fell to Earth at Grootfontein in South Africa. Discovered in 1920, it measures 2.75 metres (9 ft) by 2.43 metres (8 ft) and is estimated to weigh about 58 tonnes (59 tons).

What is a meteorite?

A meteorite is a chunk of iron or rock which falls to Earth from space. Because they are much bigger than meteors, meteorites do not burn up completely when they enter the Earth's atmosphere. They vary in size and weight.

What is a meteor?

Meteors are small particles or fragments of comets that burn up as they enter the Earth's atmosphere. They can be seen in the night sky and are often called shooting stars.

What is the greenhouse effect?

The Earth is warmed by the sun. Some of the heat is then given out by the planet in the form of infra-red radiation. Normally this would disappear into space, but gases we produce (like petrol fumes) have created an invisible barrier around our atmosphere and some of the infra-red heat cannot get through it. As a result the heat stays in our atmosphere and, according to some scientists, is making our planet permanently warmer. It is thought this will eventually lead to a change in the Earth's climate, possibly causing the polar regions to melt!

What caused a large crater in Siberia?

In 1908 a large asteroid, believed to be the size of a football pitch, exploded 8 kilometres (5 miles) above Siberia. It shattered some 1800 kilometres squared (695 sq. miles) of trees and set fire to the clothes of people over 400 kilometres (248 miles) away. The shock waves were felt as far away as London.

What are black holes?

The largest stars in the universe (much bigger than our own sun) do not die out over a period of millions of years like those of a smaller mass - they end their lives in an immense nuclear explosion. Known as 'supernovae', they occur when the gravity of the star becomes so great that it 'collapses' in on itself. However, with some stars the gravity is so powerful that it goes on collapsing endlessly, crushing the matter within it. The density of this body goes on increasing and the force of gravity keeps rising until absolutely nothing can escape - not even light - resulting in a 'black hole'. Anything that falls within this object's gravity-pull cannot escape. Although they are invisible, black holes can be detected by X-ray satellites and the first known black hole was detected in the constellation Cygnus in 1972.

Why is the sea blue?

There are several factors that affect the colour of the sea. On a bright summer day, the sea usually appears blue because it reflects the colour of the sky. If the day is overcast, then the sea appears to be black or grey. If you are near the shore, the sea bed will also influence the colour you see. The amount of salt in the water is another influence - the saltier the water the more blue the sea.

Which is the deepest lake?

It is Lake Baikal in Siberia, which reaches a depth of over 1,700 metres (5,577 ft). As the lake is so deep it also holds the most water, even more than Lake Superior.

Where is the highest mountain in the world?

Mount Everest, in the Himalayas. It has two peaks, one of which is a spectacular 8.872 metres (29,108 ft) high.

What is the longest river?

The Nile River of north-eastern Africa reaches a length of 6,670 kilometres (4,145 miles).

What is a tsunami?

A tsunami is a gigantic sea wave common in the Pacific Ocean. Special warning systems have been set up to warn fisherman and sailors when a tsunami is approaching.

What is the highest mountain in Britain?

Ben Nevis, in the highlands region of Scotland, reaches a height of 1,343 metres (4,406 ft).

What shape is a snowflake?

The amazing thing about snowflakes is that every one is a different shape! All snow-flakes are six-sided and formed of intricate patterns, but they are all different.

Which is the biggest lake in the world?

Lake Superior, one of the Great Lakes of North America, is the largest freshwater lake in the world. It covers more than 83,000 square kilometres (some 32,000 sq. miles), and about 200 different rivers flow into it.

What is the highest waterfall?

It is Angel Falls in Venezuela, South America. It measures almost 1,000 metres (3,000 ft) in height.

Which volcano has the biggest crater?

Mount Aso in Japan has a circumference of 114 kilometres (71 miles), and it measures 27 kilometres (17 miles) from north to south and 16 kilometres (10 miles) from east to west.

Where is the highest volcano?

Cerro Aconcagua in Argentina, with a height of 6,960 metres (22,834 ft), is the highest extinct volcano in the world. Of the dormant volcanoes, Volcan Llullaillaco, on the border of Argentina and Chile, is the highest at 6,723 metres (22,057 ft). Argentina also has the highest active volcano, Volcan Antofalla, which is 6,450 metres (21,161 ft) high.

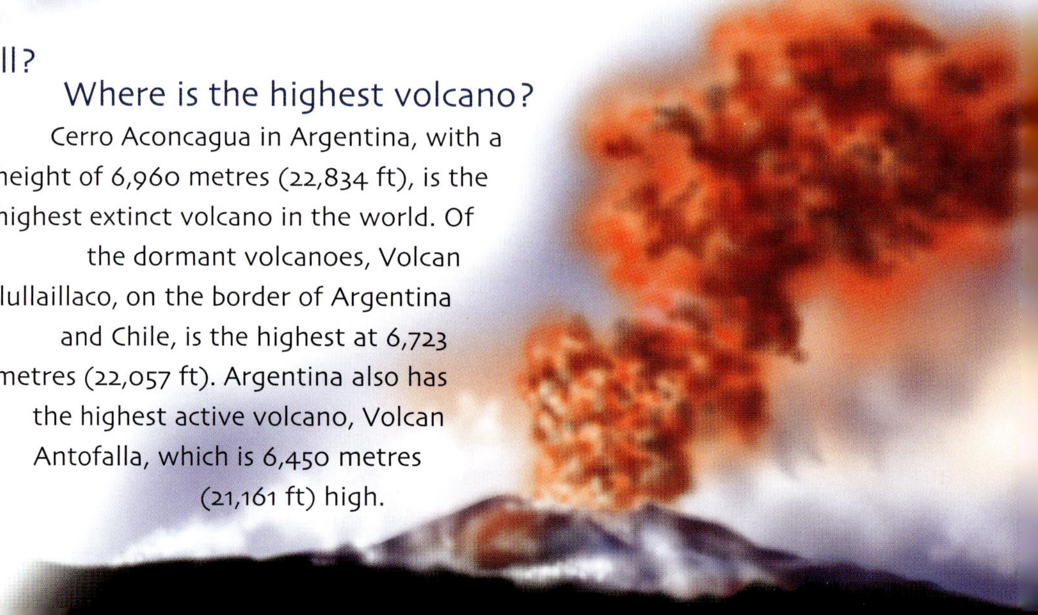

What are Singing Sands?

There are over 100 sandy areas of the world that give out musical notes or eerie squeals when someone walks over them. The sounds vary, as do the explanations for their occurrence. In Afghanistan, it is believed the drum-like noises in the sands of Reg Ruwan are caused by ghostly horsemen shoeing their horses in an underground cave. The noises heard on a beach in Hawaii are said to be the cries of the dead, although some people say the sounds are more like the baying of hounds. There are also singing sands in the British Isles, some of the most famous are at Studland Bay in Dorset, Bamburgh in Northumberland, Forth Oer in North Wales and Eigg in the Hebrides. The reason for the noises has never been satisfactorily explained. It is, however, generally accepted that as someone walks over sand, any sounds are the result of air rushing in to fill tiny spaces between the grains.

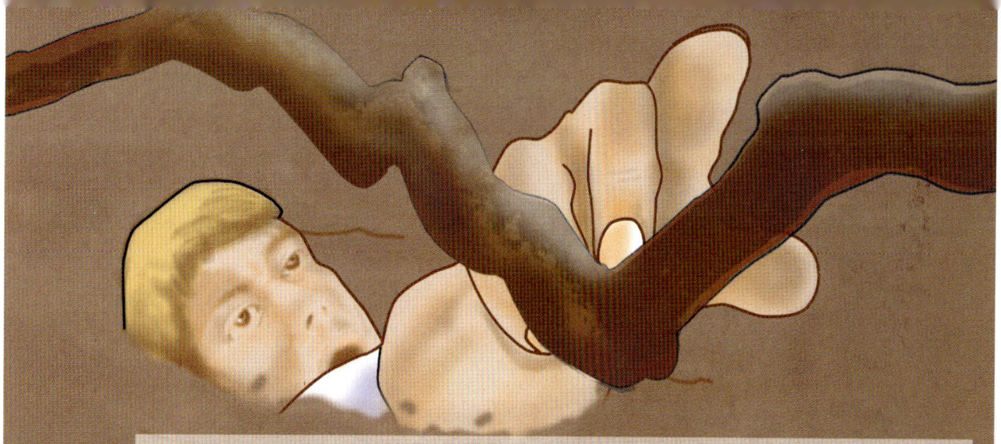

What is quicksand?

Quicksand is a mixture of sand and water that is usually found at the mouth of a river. Beneath it may be a layer of clay which stops the water draining away, leaving the sand loosely suspended. It is not true that people who step into quicksand will inevitably be sucked down until they disappear. In fact they should be able to remain afloat more easily than they do in water, as the sand will give the body more support than just water alone.

Mythology & Legends

What is the legend of Lorelei?

The legend of Lorelei tells of a young German girl who drowned herself in the River Rhine, because her lover had been unfaithful to her. She became a temptress and sat on the rocks combing her long hair and singing. Passing sailors were so enraptured by her they forgot to look where they were going, and their boats were dashed against the rock that now bears her name.

Who holds the world on his shoulders?

Greek mythology states that a race of giants called the Titans once ruled the world. When they were conquered by the god Zeus, a giant called Atlas was condemned to hold the world on his shoulders.

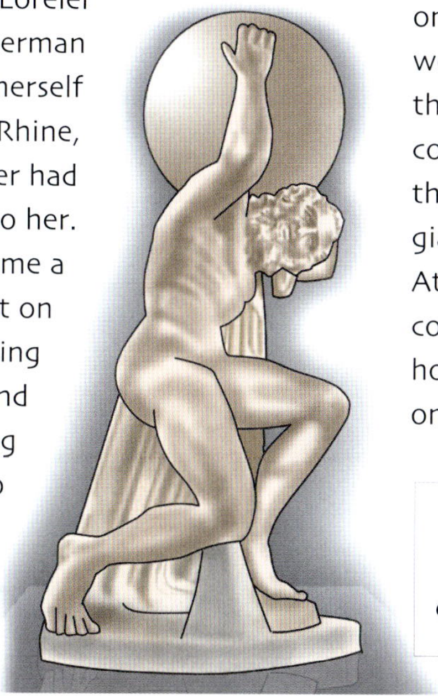

Why do we blow out birthday candles?

When you blow out the candles on a birthday cake you are following a custom created by the ancient Greeks. On the sixth day of each month, the birthday of Artemis (goddess of the hunt), the ancient Greeks made a honey cake topped with burning candles in her honour. As each candle was extinguished, the people prayed to the goddess for a present. In the same way, a person who blows out all the candles on a birthday cake, it is believed, will have a wish granted.

Who was Cupid?

Cupid was the Roman god of love. His equivalent in Greek mythology was Eros.

What was Atlantis?

According to legend, Atlantis was a beautiful city that sank beneath the sea. For many centuries people have tried to confirm if the story is true or not. Remains of ancient cities have been found under the sea but whether or not any were part of Atlantis is unknown.

Weather

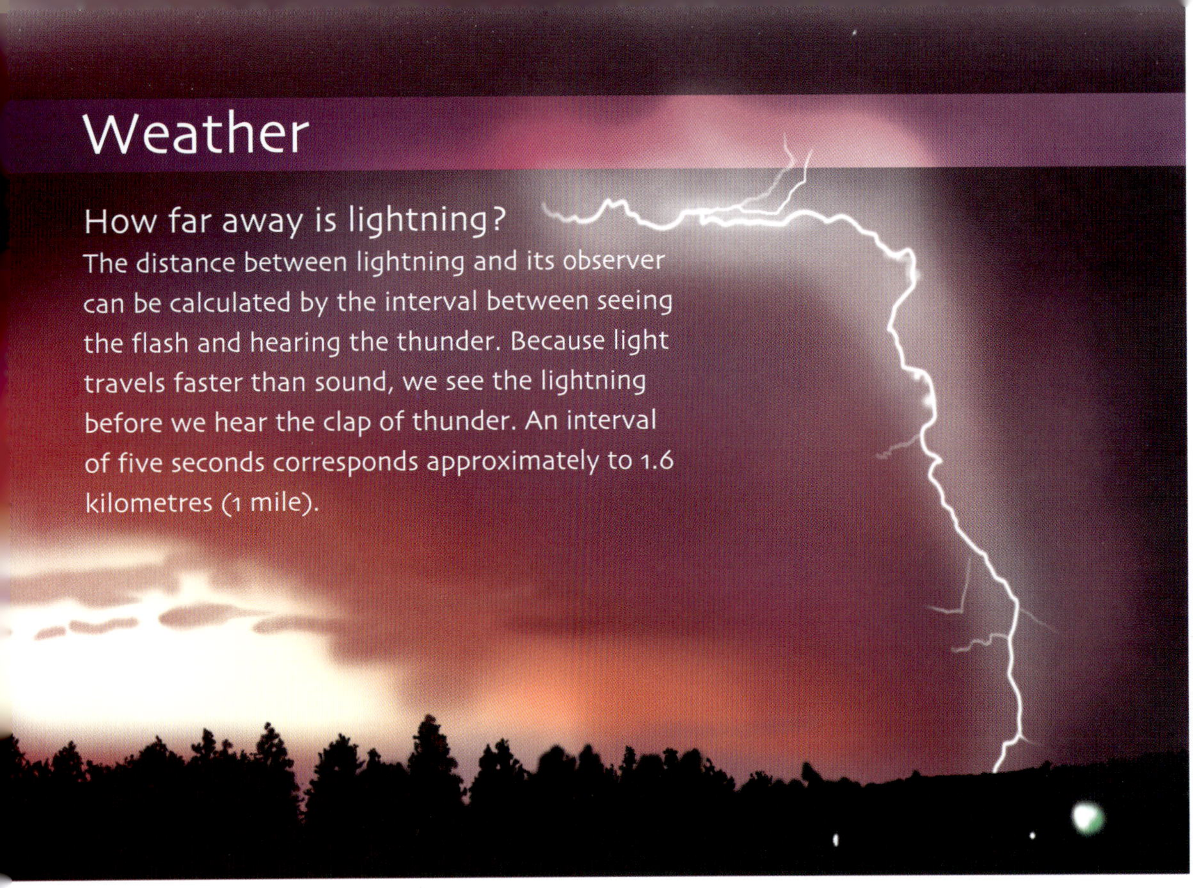

How far away is lightning?

The distance between lightning and its observer can be calculated by the interval between seeing the flash and hearing the thunder. Because light travels faster than sound, we see the lightning before we hear the clap of thunder. An interval of five seconds corresponds approximately to 1.6 kilometres (1 mile).

What are isobars?

Isobars are found on weather maps and connect places with the same barometric pressure.

What causes thunder?

Thunder is caused by the sudden heating and expanding of the air, followed by a rapid cooling and contraction when lightning flashes. This causes the air to vibrate. The rumbling sound comes from echoes rebounding from the Earth's surface or from clouds. A long roll of thunder occurs because the sound from different parts of the electrical discharge reaches the observer at different times.

What causes lightning?

Lightning is simply a large electrical spark. It is caused by electric charges jumping from one cloud to another, or from a cloud to the Earth. This occurs because different positive and negative charges are created between clouds, or between clouds and the ground, during a storm. When the difference becomes too great, a discharge of electricity occurs, resulting in a gigantic flash.

How does it rain?

If a cloud starts to cool, its vapour condenses, forming the droplets. They grow larger and larger, until they are too heavy to be held up by air currents, then they fall to the ground as rain.

Why does milk sour in a thunderstrom?

Micro-organisms called bacteria lactis are found in milk. Warm weather increases the growth rate of these bacteria. These organisms produce lactic acid, too much of which causes the casein and lime salts in the milk to separate - a state we term 'curdling' - and the milk goes sour.

How are clouds formed?

When warm air rises and reaches a particular height, it begins to cool and this causes some of the water vapour in the atmosphere to condense into droplets. A cloud is simply a large number of these droplets and is kept up in the sky by the air currents.

Who invented the lightning conductor?

The lightning conductor was invented by Benjamin Franklin. It is a rod of metal attached to the top of a tall building so the lightning does not hit the building itself.

Why did Benjamin Franklin fly a kite during a thunderstorm?

In 1752 the great American statesman and scientist attached a key to the end of a kite line and flew the kite during a thunderstorm. The key gave off sparks when lightning struck, thus proving that lightning is an electrical discharge. It was a very dangerous experiment and people have been killed trying to copy it.

Calendar Facts

What are the Ides of March?

In the Roman calendar, the Ides were the 13th or 15th day of the month. The Ides of March, however, are still remembered because Julius Caesar was killed on that day. He was warned by a fortune teller to "Beware the Ides of March" and was stabbed at a meeting of the Roman senate on 15th March 44 BC.

What are the months of the year named after?

The origins of the calendar months go back to the time of the ancient Romans. The names are Latin in origin, some in honour of famous people and some according to the order in which the months occur. This last method of naming has left us with a rather curious result: September, October, November and December are the 9th, 10th, 11th, and 12th months but their names come from Latin words meaning 7th, 8th, 9th and 10th. This happened because at one time the Roman calendar had only ten months and began with March. Around 700 BC the calendar was reformed and two months added at the beginning of the year, January and February. January is named after the god Janus, who had two faces and looked two ways at once: backwards at the old year and forwards to the new. Another god, Februus, gave us the name for February. March took its name from Mars, the god of war. April came from Latin word aperture, meaning an opening, signifying the month in which plants open and grow after winter. The origins of May and June are less certain. May was probably named after the goddess Maia, whose name meant 'nurse' or 'mother'. June may have connections with Juno, the goddess of women. July and August are named in honour of famous Romans: July for Julius Caesar and August for Augustus Caesar, the first Roman emperor.

Why does February have 29 days in a leap year?

About 2000 years ago Julius Caesar reorganised the calendar by adding an extra day every fourth year, following the advice of the Greek astronomer Sosigenes. This was necessary because the Earth takes 365 days, 5 hours, 48 minutes and 46 seconds to travel around the Sun. The Romans had found that, with a year being only 365 days, festivals did not keep in line with the seasons. In 1582 Pope Gregory XIII made the system more accurate by ruling that the century years (eg: 1700, 1800, 1900, etc.) should not be treated as leap years unless they were divisible by 400. So there was not a 29th February in 1900 but there was one in the year 2000.

Thor, the God of thunder

How were the days named?

Four of the names we use for the days of the week are of Scandinavian origin, while the others come from heavenly bodies. Sunday is named in honour of the Sun; Monday was the day of the Moon; Tuesday was the day of Tiw, the Scandinavian god of war; Wednesday comes from Woden (Odin), chief of the Scandinavian gods; Thursday is named after Thor, the god of thunder; Freya (or Frigga), the goddess of friendship, gave her name to Friday; and Saturday was the day of Saturn.

Why are there 24 hours in a day?

The ancient Egyptians divided daytime into ten parts marked on a sundial. At night they divided the stars into twelve groups that appeared in the night sky one after the other. Neither of these methods of calculating time was suitable at dawn or dusk, so these were added to the 22 divisions to make a total of 24. The system has also been traced to the Babylonians, who are thought to have been the first to divide daylight into 12 hours, a similar division being applied to the period of darkness.

What was the first boat?

It is thought a log hollowed out by fire or with a stone axe was Man's first proper boat. Early Man also lashed logs together with vines to make rafts. Initially, hands were used as oars, but it was soon discovered that wood was far more effective.

What is Davy Jones' locker?

When sailors say that someone has 'gone to Davy Jones' locker', it means they have drowned. Davy Jones' locker is the ocean itself and Davy Jones is regarded as one of the spirits of the sea. It is thought the name 'Jones' came from the biblical story of Jonah, who was swallowed by a whale. It is possible the name 'Davy' came from the West Indian word 'duppy', meaning 'devil'.

Who invented the hovercraft?

The hovercraft was invented by Christopher Cokerell. To try out his theories, his first test model was made from a tin can, a coffee tin and a hairdryer.

What happened to the Mary Celeste?

On 5th December 1872, the two-masted ship the Mary Celeste was found adrift in the Atlantic. Everything was as it should be. The sails were fine. There was plenty of fresh water and food on board and the cargo was still in the hold - but there was no-one on board. The ship was completely deserted. Breakfast was laid out on the table in the captain's cabin but it looked as if it had been abandoned halfway through. To this day no-one knows for certain what happened to all those on board.

Why is a ship's speed measured in knots?

A knot is the speed of one nautical mile per hour. In days gone by, the speed of a ship was measured by letting out a rope attached to a log. There were knots along the rope and a sailor would count these as he allowed the rope to slip through his hands. The ship's speed was the number of knots passed within a given time.

What is a nautical mile?

A nautical or sea mile is slightly longer than a land mile. It measures 1,852 metres (approximately 2,025 yds).

What was the first steam vessel to cross the Atlantic?

The first steam-powered vessel to cross the Atlantic was the Savannah in 1819. However, it used steam power only for the start and finish of the journey, relying on sails for the rest of the voyage. Nineteen years later, the Sirius became the first ship to make the entire Atlantic crossing using steam.

Why is a ship's log book so called?

When the distance a ship has travelled is calculated from the line of knots, it is entered in a log book, named because of the log at the end of the line.

What are flotsam and jetsam?

Both words refer to wreckage or other property floating in the sea. The difference between them is that 'flotsam' are items floating on the surface accidentally, whereas 'jetsam' are items that have been deliberately thrown overboard to lighten a sinking ship.

What was the Spanish Armada?

A fleet of 130 ships, sent to England in 1588 by King Philip II of Spain. The main purpose was to spread the Roman Catholic religion. The king was also afraid that England was too strong, putting the land he owned in the Netherlands under threat. Lastly, it was a chance for the Spanish to get revenge on the English, who had been attacking Spanish treasure ships the world over.

Who was the first person to fly across the Atlantic?

Actually there were two people: Captain John Alcock and Lieutenant Arthur Whitten-Brown. In 1913 the newspaper publisher Lord Northcliffe offered a prize of £10,000 for the first non-stop flight across the Atlantic Ocean. As it was only four years after the first flight across the English Channel, an Atlantic flight of 3,060 kms (1,901 miles) was thought to be impossible - especially as aircraft at the time had a top range of only 1,500 kilometres (932 miles)!

At the end of the First World War, aeronautical engineers began seriously considering the Atlantic challenge. A chief test pilot, John Alcock, had given the problem a great deal of thought while a prisoner of war. By chance he met Arthur Whitten-Brown who, while in hospital during the war, had studied aerial navigation. They both took off from Newfoundland, Canada, in June 1919, in their plane powered by two Rolls Royce engines. After a hazardous journey they crashed into an Irish bog, gaining a permanent place in the history of aviation.

Who invented the jet plane?

The idea of jet propulsion was first proposed early in the 20th century. Frank Whittle, an officer cadet at RAF Cranwell, formulated the theory of jet-powered flight. It was not, however, until 1929 that he solved the basic problems associated with high-speed flying. He applied for a patent in 1930 and, on 12th April 1937, he saw the first test-bed run of his jet engine. Development continued over the following years but, in spite of this pioneering work, Whittle was not the first to get a jet aeroplane off the ground. The first jet-powered flight was made by a Heinkel He 178 at Marienehe, Germany, in August 1939, with an engine designed by Dr Hans von Ohain.

Who were Wilbur and Orville Wright?

They were two American brothers who designed and flew the first powered aircraft, in 1903.

Why are ships launched with champagne?

Launching a ship by breaking a bottle of champagne or wine across the bows is said to be the modern equivalent of an ancient sacrifice to the gods. In times gone by, the blood of an animal, or even human blood, was often used for this purpose in the hope that the gods would be so pleased with the gift, they would protect the ship at all times.

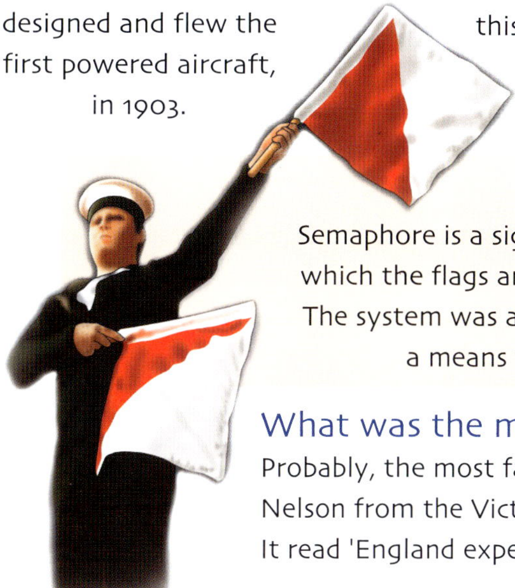

What is Semaphore?

Semaphore is a signalling system using two flags. The ways in which the flags are held represent the letters of the alphabet. The system was adopted by the British navy in about 1816, as a means for ships to communicate with one another.

What was the most famous flag signal ever flown?

Probably, the most famous flag signal was that flown by Admiral Nelson from the Victory before the Battle of Trafalgar in 1805. It read 'England expects that every man will do his duty'.

When was a coconut used to launch a ship?

In 1937 the 4,000 tonne passenger vessel El Medina was launched at Glasgow by the High Commissioner for India. To launch the ship he used a coconut, rather than champagne, as the ship would be carrying Mohammedan pilgrims, whose religion forbids the consumption of alcohol.

Who was the first man to fly solo around the world?

Wiley Hardemann Post. He took off from Floyd Bennett Field, New York, on 15th July 1933. He returned to the same airfield on 22nd July, having covered 25,099 kilometres (15,596 miles) in a flying time of 115 hours, 26 minutes.

How do ships use flags to send messages?

There is an international code for the different coloured and patterned flags flown by ships. Messages can be sent from ship to ship, or ship to shore, by flying the flags in order. Some individual flags also mean particular messages as well as representing a letter.

Architectural Landmarks

When was Tutankhamen's tomb discovered?

In 1922, the English archeologist Howard Carter was excavating in the Valley of the Kings at Thebes, in Egypt. On 4th November, some steps were discovered and later investigation revealed these to be the entrance to the tomb of Tutankhamen.

Where is the oldest bridge?

It is thought the clapper bridges (made of large stones placed on boulders) on Exmoor and Dartmoor, are of prehistoric origin - but none can be dated with any certainty. The oldest bridge that can be dated is a stone arch bridge in Izmir, Turkey, which was built almost 3,000 years ago.

What was the original purpose of London's Marble Arch?

Marble Arch was first built as the main entrance to Buckingham Palace. However, it was not wide enough for a stagecoach to get through, so it was moved to its present site near Hyde Park.

How did the White House get its name?

Washington, USA, was captured by British forces during the Anglo-American War of 1812 and many buildings were burned. One such building was the President's mansion. To conceal the damage, the building was given a quick coat of whitewash. The Presidential residence has been known as the White House ever since.

What was the original purpose of the London Monument?

This tall column was designed by Christopher Wren. It commemorates the Great Fire of London of 1666, although it was originally intended to be a telescope. The column was built to house a large lens presented to the Royal Academy by the Dutch scientist Christiaan Huygens but the tube was too short. Wren then built a staircase inside and it became the London Monument!

What is the Acropolis?

The word 'acropolis' is Greek for the upper part of a town, often a fortress on the top of a hill. Many towns had an acropolis but today the name usually refers to just one - the Acropolis in Athens - parts of which, dating from the 5th century BC, remain to this day.

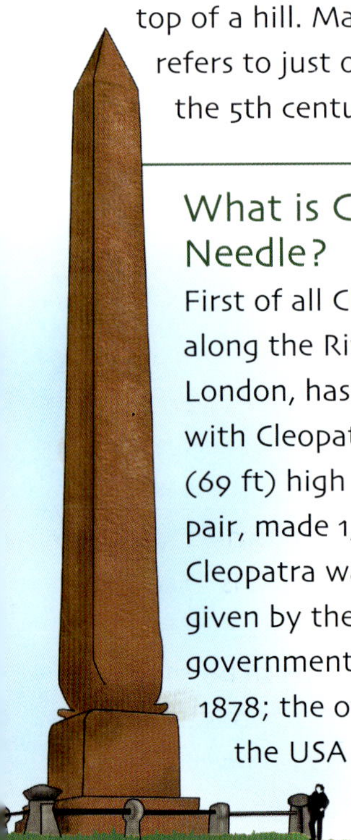

What is Cleopatra's Needle?

First of all Cleopatra's Needle, along the River Thames in London, has nothing to do with Cleopatra! The 21 metre (69 ft) high pillar is one of a pair, made 1,500 years before Cleopatra was born. One was given by the Egyptian government to Britain in 1878; the other was given to the USA and is in Central Park, New York.

What is the largest inhabited castle in the world?

Windsor Castle in England. Much of it was built in the 11th century by William the Conqueror and it is now the official home of the British monarch.

What is unusual about Haydn's Tomb?

The tomb of the famous composer Franz Joseph Haydn lies at Eisenstadt, Austria. It is unusual because the composer's body is not in it. His body lies in the crypt of the church and his skull is at the museum in Vienna.

How high is the Monument?

It is thought that the height of the Monument, 62 metres (203 ft), is exactly the same as the distance from its base to the site where the Great Fire began.

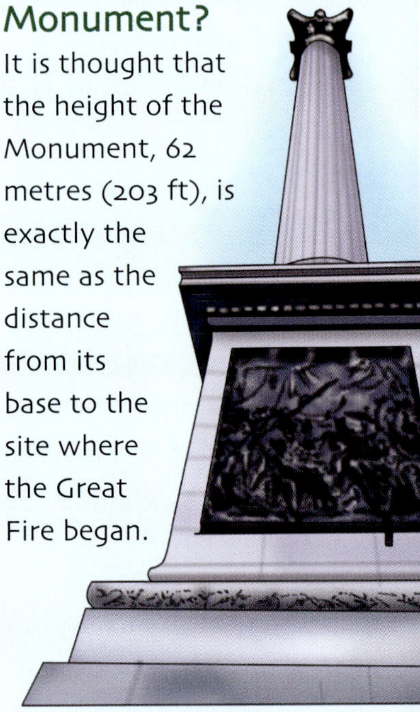

Could the tunnel collapse?

The tunnel is lined with reinforced concrete that can withstand the force of a bomb or an earthquake, so there is no chance of it collapsing. The tunnel lining is made with rings of concrete 45 centimetres (18 in) in thickness.

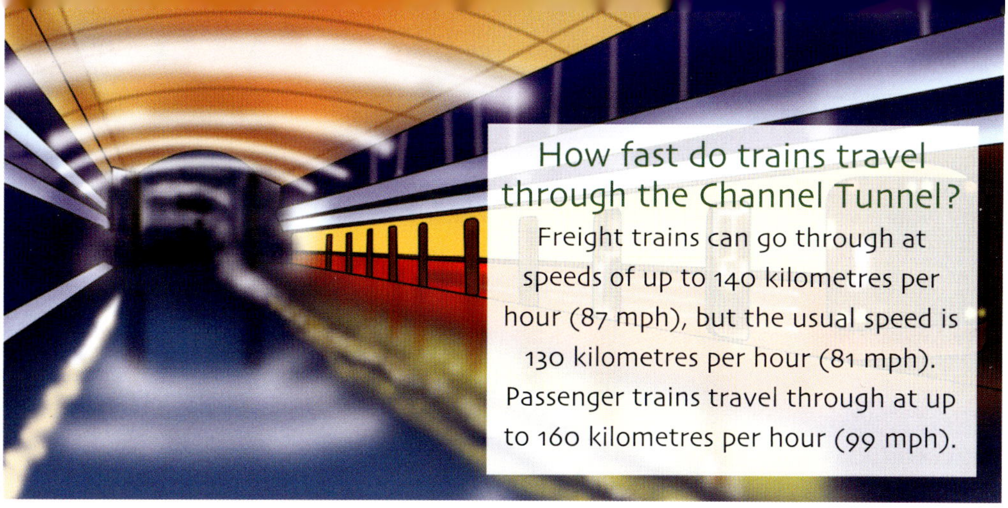

How fast do trains travel through the Channel Tunnel?

Freight trains can go through at speeds of up to 140 kilometres per hour (87 mph), but the usual speed is 130 kilometres per hour (81 mph). Passenger trains travel through at up to 160 kilometres per hour (99 mph).

When was the Channel Tunnel opened?

The official opening took place on 6th May 1994.

How deep is the Channel Tunnel?

There are actually three tunnels: two single-track rail tunnels and one two-track service tunnel. The three tunnels run for 50 kilometres (31 miles), and run between 23 metres (75 ft) to 46 metres (151 ft) below the sea.

Who built the Sphinx?

Egypt has many statues of sphinxes. These represent imaginary animals with a lion's body and the head of a man. They were built as shrines to Egyptian gods. The most famous sphinx lies at Giza and was built on the orders of King Khafra in about 2,600 BC.

Where is the Bridge of Sighs?

The Bridge of Sighs is a famous covered bridge in Venice. It crosses the Rio di Palazzo and joins the Doges' Palace with the old state prison. Its name comes from the sadness of the prisoners as they walked to their cells.

Who had a palace of ice?

In 1739, Empress Anna of Russia had a novel palace built - it was made entirely of ice.

Construction Material

How is concrete delivered ready-mixed?

The various ingredients of cement are loaded into a large mixer on the back of a lorry. As a lorry is driven to a building site, the mixer rotates and mixes the ingredients - sand, cement, gravel and water. By the time the lorry arrives at the site, the concrete is ready for use.

How are bricks made?

There are three basic ways in which bricks can be made. In the first, water is mixed with clay into a paste which is forced into wooden moulds. The mixture is then tipped out and placed in giant ovens called kilns. The second method involves forming a very stiff clay mixture which is forced through a rectangular hole before being cut into brick-sized pieces with a wire. The third method is similar to the first, but less water is used and the bricks are pressed into shape. The first process is known as the 'stock method' because the wooden moulds are called stocks; the second is known as the 'wire-cut' process; and the third is called the 'semi-dry' process.

Once the bricks are moulded into shape, they are placed in kilns to be fired, a process that takes several days, during which the bricks are subjected to a very high temperature. Most modern brick manufacturers use a continuous chamber kiln through which the bricks travel, so that by the time they come out from the other end of the kiln, they have been completely fired and are ready for use.

Why do bricks overlap?

If you look at a brick building, you will see that the bricks are not laid directly on top of one another. If they were, the building would soon fall down! Bricks are overlapped so that each brick supports its neighbours and there are no continuous vertical joins.

Law & Administration

Is fingerprinting a modern technique?

No. The ancient Chinese used fingerprinting as a means of identification. The ancient Babylonians made fingerprints in clay.

Who first suggested using fingerprints to catch criminals?

Henry Faulds, a Scottish physician, in a letter he had published in Nature magazine in October 1880.

Which is the world's oldest parliament?

The Althing is the parliament of Iceland. It has been in existence since the 10th century making it the oldest parliament in history.

What is Hansard?

Hansard is the name given to the official reports of events in the House of Commons. It gets its name from Luke Hansard, who started a House of Commons Journal in 1774.

What was 'hue and cry'?

In Anglo-Saxon times official police forces, like we have today, had yet to be formed.It was therefore the duty of each person to raise a 'hue and cry' if he or she saw a crime being committed. When that happened everyone had to stop what they were doing and chase the criminal. This system continued in Britain with very little change until well into the 17th century.

What was the Nose Tax?

No, it was not a tax on people's noses! It was a tax of one ounce of gold to be paid by every householder in Ireland during the 9th century. The tax was successfully levied by the Danes for 13 years until the officials were massacred. The tax obtained its curious name because anyone who refused or was unable to pay the tax had his nose slit in punishment.

What was the gunpowder plot?

It was a plan to blow up British Parliament on the first day of a new session, when King James I and all his ministers would be present. The plot was designed to be the start of an armed uprising against the persecution of Catholics in England. The plot failed because one of the conspirators, Francis Tresham, warned a friend not to attend Parliament on that day and all the plotters were arrested.

What is a democracy?

Democracy is a form of government in which the people of a country decide future events. This is usually done by the population electing persons to represent their views in the government. The word comes from two Greek words 'demos' (people) and 'kratos' (power). The former American president Abraham Lincoln described it as government of the people, by the people and for the people".

Who were the Bow Street Runners?

Established in 1749, by the novelist Henry Fielding, the Bow Street Runners were a group of law officers attached to Bow Street court in London As they wore scarlet waistcoats, they were nicknamed Robin Redbreasts. Police forces as we know them today did not yet exist. The Bow Street Runners thus created a new respect for law and order and had considerable success in catching wrong-doers.

Which British Prime Minister was assassinated?

Spencer Perceval, elected in 1809. Three years later, he was walking through the House of Commons when he was shot dead by John Bellingham, who had a grudge against the government.

What was the Window Tax?

It was a tax, first levied in 1696, on the number of windows in a house. The tax remained in force until 1851, although the number of windows liable to tax varied. People who did not want to pay simply bricked up some of their windows, which can still be seen on some old houses today.

What is woolsack?

The woolsack is the seat of the Lord Chancellor, used when he is presiding over the sittings of the House of Lords in London. At an early date, a sack of wool was used as a seat. During the reign of Henry VIII, the Chancellor and other high officials sat upon such sacks. Today, the woolsack is a large square cushion of wool, covered with red cloth. The use of the woolsack for this purpose reflects the vital part which the wool trade once played in the British economy.

War

How did a bucket start a war?

In the year 1325, a group of men from the state of Modena, Italy, stole a wooden bucket from the state of Bologna. This resulted in a fight between the two groups that developed into a 12 year war.

Why do soldiers salute?

In the Middle Ages, it was the custom for knights in armour to raise their visors when meeting someone, as a sign of respect and friendship. Although modern soldiers do not have visors like the knights of old, the salute is still performed as a sign of respect.

What was the Maginot Line?

Named after Andre Maginot (French Minister of War), this line of fortifications was built between 1929 and 1934 along the French border with Luxembourg and Switzerland. When the Germans invaded France in 1940, they entered through Belgium, a region not protected by the Maginot Line.

Who invented the cannon?

The exact origin of the cannon is unclear, but it is almost certain it was developed in Europe. The earliest references to such a weapon date from the early 14th century. The first important use of cannon in warfare was at the Battle of Crecy and the siege of Calais in 1346-47.

What were early cannons made of?

The barrels of early cannons were made of wood and leather strengthened by iron bands. They fired stone cannon balls.

Which is the oldest army?

The oldest army in the world is that of the Swiss Guard in the Vatican City, Rome, Italy. Its origins date back to at least the 15th century

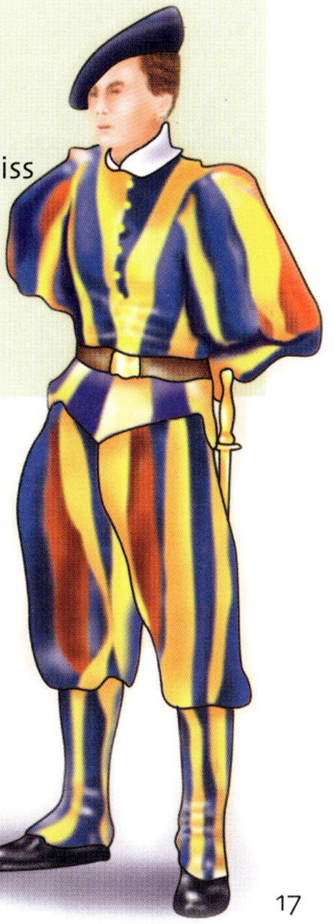

How did a football match start a war?

The supporters of El Salvador and Honduras began fighting each other during a football match in 1969. The brawl was quite serious, and developed rapidly into full scale war between the two countries.

What was 'The War of Jenkins' Ear'?

On 9th April 1731, Spanish coastguards boarded the ship Rebecca off the coast of Havana, Cuba. They cut off the ear of the captain, Robert Jenkins, and tied him to the mast before setting the ship adrift. In 1738, he told his story to the British House of Commons and it provided an excuse for a naval war with Spain which lasted from 1739 to 1742. This became known as 'The War of Jenkins' Ear'.

What was the mutiny on the Bounty?

In 1787, Captain William Bligh commanded HMS Bounty to the South Pacific. He was so strict the crew mutinied, setting him adrift with 18 men. The mutineers settled in Tahiti and on Pitcairn Island, where some of their descendants live to this day.

Who led the mutiny on the Bounty?

Fletcher Christian the mate on HMS Bounty, led the mutiny against the harsh regime of Captain Bligh. After the mutiny, Christian settled on Pitcairn Island in the Pacific.

What happened to Captain Bligh?

After being cast adrift by the crew, Bligh and his supporters sailed 5,822 kilometres (3,618 miles) to Timor Island, near Java. They managed this without charts and very little food. On his return to England, Bligh reported the mutiny. In 1805 he was appointed Governor of New South Wales, Australia, where once again, his strict discipline caused a mutiny in 1808. On returning to England, he was made an admiral.

How did a cockerel help win a battle?

During the battle of St Vincent in 1797, the British ship HMS Marlborough was so badly damaged, the officers considered surrendering. The captain and the lieutenant had been wounded and the ship dismasted. Then a shot from the Spanish fleet hit the kitchen coop on board. A cockerel found sudden freedom, fluttered over what was left of the damaged mainmast and gave a hearty crow. The ship's company responded with three loud cheers, and with their morale heightened went back into action with renewed vigour.

What is the shortest war on record?

At 9.02 am on 27th August 1896, Britain declared war on Zanzibar. After just 38 minutes of bombardment the Sultan of Zanzibar surrendered.

How was a city saved by a bowl of soup?

During the siege of Geneva, Switzerland, in the 16th century, a housewife heard the enemy climbing the city walls. She prevented them from entering the city by pouring a cauldron of boiling soup over them.

Where is the Mason-Dixon line?

The Mason-Dixon Line is a boundary that separated the northern and southern states before the American Civil War. It was established by the Penn family, of Pennsylvania and the Calvert family, who owned Maryland. The two families argued continually about where the boundary should be. Eventually, they agreed to employ two Englishmen, Charles Mason and Jeremiah Dixon, to survey the boundary. The work was finished in 1767, and still exists as the boundary between the states of Maryland, Pennsylvania and part of West Virginia.

What is the longest war on record?

The Hundred Years' War, which began between France and England in 1337. It is known as 'The Hundred Years' War' but it actually lasted 116 years!

Historical Events

What was the Boston tea party?

When the British imposed taxes on tea imported by America in the 18th century, the people of Boston decided to refuse delivery of the goods. But when the tea ships would not leave, the Bostonians took drastic action. After dusk on 16th December 1773, a band of men disguised as Native Americans slipped aboard the ships in Boston Harbor, broke open the tea chests and threw all the tea into the water.

When was the RNLI founded?

The RNLI was formed in 1824 when a meeting in London resolved " . . . that an institution be now formed for the Preservation of Life in cases of Shipwreck on the Coasts of the United Kingdom, to be supported by donations and annual subscription; and to be called the National Institution for the Preservation of Life from Shipwreck." The name was changed to the Royal National Lifeboat Institution 30 years later.

How did the great fire of London start?

On 2nd September 1666, a small fire was discovered in a wooden house in Pudding Lane. The house belonged to the King's baker, John Farynore. It raged on for four days and destroyed a vast area of London.

How many people died in the great fire of London?

Thankfully, although a vast area of the city was destroyed, only six people were killed in the fire.

When did a horse choose a king?

In AD 522 Persia was left without a king after the death of Cambyses. Various contenders for the crown decided to meet on horseback at sunrise - the man whose horse neighed first would become king. One such contender was Darius Hystaspes, whose groom took his horse to the meeting spot and allowed it to become fond of a mare that was grazing there. The next day, Darius' horse immediately neighed for the mare - and Darius was chosen as king.

Which British institution began in a coffee house?

In 1698 the London dealers in company stocks and shares arranged to meet in Jonathan's Coffee House. It was the start of what was to become the London Stock Exchange. As a result of this unusual first meeting place, the messengers in the Stock Exchange are still called 'waiters'.

When did Prince Charles become the Prince of Wales?

In 1958, when he was almost ten. Charles was invested at Caernafon Castle on 1st July 1969. He is the 21st heir apparent to bear the title.

What was the Magna Carta?

'Magna Carta' is Latin for 'Great Charte'. It was a document approved by King John at Runnymede in 1215. Because of the cruel manner in which he treated the English people and his demand for money to help fight his wars, King John was not popular. The Barons were particularly against the king because he demanded large payments from them. Eventually they revolted and drew up an agreement which the king accepted. This document, the Articles of the Barons, was converted into a Royal Charter which was sent to the sheriff of every county in the land. Commonly known as the Magna Carta, it had a great influence on history and marked the first steps to constitutional government - a government according to law.

Amazing People

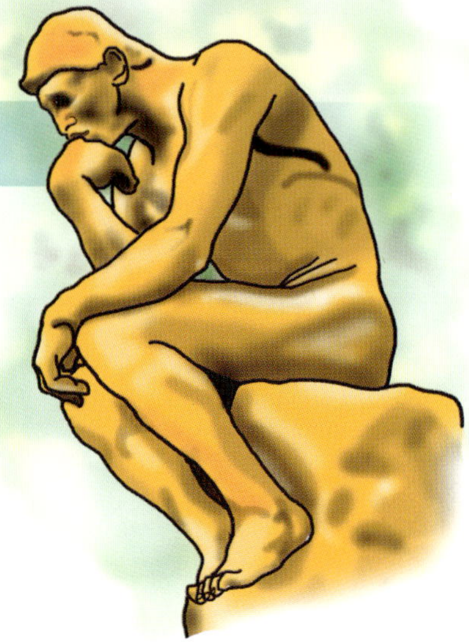

For what was Rodin famous?

Auguste Rodin was born in Paris in 1840. He was a sculptor famous for such works as The Thinker and The Kiss.

Why do people sometimes shout 'Geronimo!' before making a great jump?

Geronimo was an American Indian chief. When escaping from the US Cavalry, he made a daring leap from a high cliff into a river. As he fell, he yelled his name. This incident was then depicted in a 1940 film and during the Second World War, American paratroopers began shouting 'Geronimo!' when they jumped.

Which US President could write two languages at the same time?

Quite a lot of people are ambidextrous meaning they can write with both their right and left hands. Some people have developed this ability so they can write with both hands at the same time. But James Abraham Garfield, President of the USA from 1880-81, took his talent one step further - he could write in Latin with one hand and in Greek with the other!

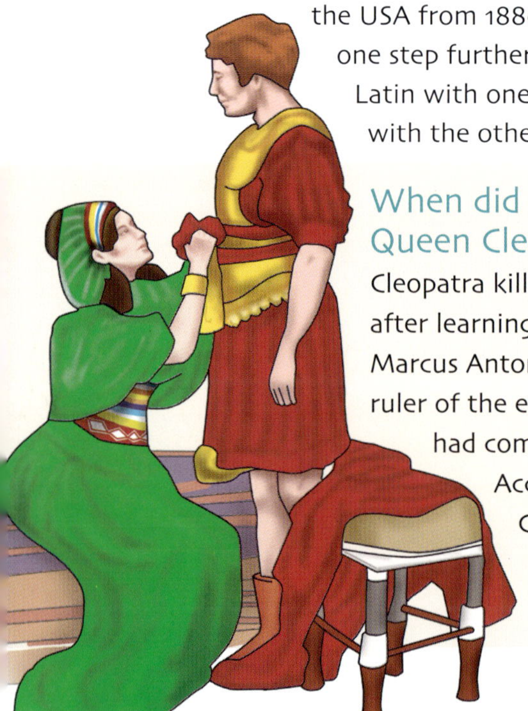

When did Queen Cleopatra die?

Cleopatra killed herself in 30 BC after learning that her lover, Marcus Antonius (Mark Anthony), ruler of the eastern Roman Empire, had committed suicide. According to tradition, Cleopatra poisoned herself by making an asp bite her.

Who was Edith Cavell?

Edith Louisa Cavell was born in Norfolk in 1865. She grew up to become a nurse and moved to Brussels in 1907. During the First World War, she and her colleague, Philippe Baucq, helped English and French soldiers escape to Holland. Cavell was arrested in 1915, and she and Baucq were condemned to death.

Who were the first known people to sail around the world?

The surviving crew of the Victoria. The vessel left Spain in 1519 and returned in 1522. Sadly, the navigator, Ferdinand Magellan, did not complete the journey. He was killed by natives in the Philippines in 1521.

Who was Guy Fawkes?

He was born in 1570. His name is remembered to this day because he was part of the Gunpowder Plot of 1605, a scheme to blow up the Houses of Parliament in London.

Who was Capability Brown?

Lancelot Brown was a famous landscape gardener of the 18th century. He was nicknamed 'Capability' because he would often say that a place had 'capabilities of improvement'.

Who was Tom Thumb?

His real name was Charles Sherwood Stratton. He was born on 4th January 1838 and died on 15th July 1883. Stratton became famous as General Tom Thumb because he was only 1 metre (about 3 ft) tall.

When did St Valentine's day customs originate?

St Valentine's Day customs originally developed from the Roman festival of Lupercalia, which took place each February.

Who was Tutankhamen?

Tutankhamen was an Egyptian pharaoh who lived from 1361 to 1352 BC. He is often called 'the boy pharaoh' because he was only nine when he became king.

Who was Confucius?

K'ung Fu-Tzu was a Chinese teacher who lived from about 551 to 479 BC. The Latin version of his name is Confucius, the name used by Jesuit missionaries in China. His teachings formed the basis of Confucianism, a guide to life followed by many people of China.

Who was Lawrence of Arabia?

T E Lawrence was a British archaeologist and soldier who worked on excavations in Egypt from 1911-14. He then became an intelligence officer in Cairo and later, joined the Arab revolt against the Turks. He lived with and dressed like the Arabs, and became known as Lawrence of Arabia.

Who was the 'Maid of Orleans'?

This was the nickname of Joan of Arc (1412-31), the young heroine who led an army that saved the town of Orleans, France, during the Hundred Years' War.

How did Joan of Arc die?

Joan was found guilty of heresy and witchcraft by the English. She was burned at the stake on 30th May 1431. In 1920, Joan was canonized, becoming Saint Joan of Arc.

Who were the Luddites?

In the early 19th century, many factory workers rioted in protest to new machinery that was replacing them in the factories. Their leader was General Ludd and the rioters became known as Luddites. However, it turned out there was no such person as General Ludd - it was just a name the rioters had made up!

Who were the Pankhursts?

Emmeline Pankhurst and her daughters, Christabel and Sylvia, were the leaders of the English suffragette movement (the fight for voting rights for women). Their campaigns were often militant and all three women were frequently arrested. The campaign was a success and women were eventually granted the right to vote.

Who was Saint Valentine?

The most likely saint after whom 'valentines' are named was a Roman priest. Under the persecution of Claudius the Goth, St. Valentine was beheaded in about 269 AD. There are three other St. Valentines, any one of whom could be the person after whom valentine cards were named. Unfortunately, none of the four had much connection with love.

Who was Mata Hari?

Mata Hari, whose real name was Margaretha Geertruida Zelle, was born in 1876. From 1905, she was a professional dancer and also acted as a spy for both the French and the Germans during the First World War.

When did Napoleon become famous?

Napoleon is now best known for his extraordinary military campaigns. Yet he was a national figure in France long before what became known as the Napoleonic Wars. He was a capable artillery commander when, in 1795, he came to the attention of the government as a man to be relied on. Appointed second-in-command of the army of the interior, he was largely responsible for crushing a royalist rising.

Who was Kublai Khan?

Kublai Khan (1215-1294), grandson of Genghis Khan, was one of the great rulers in world history. When his brother died in 1259, he became the great emperor of the Mongol Empire. By 1279, he had conquered the entire country. He tried to expand his empire to include Java and Japan but his invasions of these countries were unsuccessful.

Who was Sitting Bull?

Sitting Bull, who also appeared in Buffalo Bill's Wild West Show, was an American Indian chief. He led the Sioux at the Battle of the Little Bighorn in 1876, where they defeated the 7th Cavalry commanded by General Custer.

Who was Buffalo Bill?

Buffalo Bill's Wild West Show was formed in 1883. It was a spectacular circus featuring cowboys and Indians who toured all over the USA and Europe. Among the stars were Annie Oakley, Sitting Bull and Buffalo Bill. Buffalo Bill claimed he had earned his nickname because he had shot over 4,000 bisons to help feed men who were building a railroad.

Who was El Cid?

Rodrigo Diaz de Vivar was born in about 1043 in Castile, Spain. He became a national hero when he fought against the Moors. He was known to Spaniards as 'el Campeador' (the champion) but the Moors called him 'el Cid' (the Lord).

Who was Annie Oakley?

Annie Oakley, who starred in Buffalo Bill's Wild West Show, was a crack shot with guns. She even beat the American marksman Frank E Butler, who later became her husband.

Who was Bonnie Prince Charlie?

When James II fled England in 1688, leaving the throne to the Protestant William of Orange, he took with him his baby son, who was then only six months old. This baby, also called James, grew up in exile, calling himself James III. It was his son, christened Charles Edward, who was the Bonnie Prince Charlie of history. He landed in Scotland in 1745 and led a rising against the reigning king, George II. When the rising was finally crushed, at Culloden in 1746, the discouraged Prince sailed away into exile.

Were there ever any female pirates?

There were quite a few well-known women pirates in the 17th century. The two most famous were Anne Bonny and Mary Read.

Who were the Tolpuddle Martyrs?

A group of six labourers from Dorset who were unhappy with their poor working conditions formed a union to improve them. Although this was not illegal, the government decided the union could lead to unrest and in 1834 they were exiled to Australia for seven years. Public opinion against the sentences proved so great that the men were pardoned in 1836.

Who was Marco Polo?

Marco Polo (1254-1324) was an Italian merchant from Venice. In 1271, he joined his father and uncle on an overland journey to the Far East. Polo ended up staying in China for 17 years, employed by the emperor, Kublai Khan, for official missions. He eventually returned to Italy by sea (1292-1295).

Who was John Bull?

John Bull was a symbol of the British people and was even a nickname for Britain itself. The name first appeared in comics after Dr John Arbuthnott published a book called The History of John Bull (1712).

Who was 'The Iron Duke'?

The Iron Duke was a nickname of the Duke of Wellington. It actually came from an iron vessel called Duke of Wellington, which was launched in Victorian times. As such metal vessels were unusual then, it was called 'The Iron Duke'.

Who was the 'Lady with the Lamp'?

This nickname was given to a nurse who tended the injured during the Crimean War which ended in 1856. She was Florence Nightingale, and was nicknamed 'The Lady with the Lamp' because she carried a lamp as she checked on her patients during the night

Interesting Inventions

What is a patent?

A patent is a licence issued by a government office to a person or company giving the right to make or sell an invention. If an inventor wants to stop other people copying his invention, he has to apply to the Patent Office with a full description of the invention. The application is then checked against the records to make sure that the idea is original, and has not been copied from another inventor.

Who invented the kite?

The first kite is said to have been invented by a Chinese farmer whose hat blew off in the wind. He tied a string to it and the next time it blew off he had a kite!

Who invented the first lock?

The first locks were invented over 4,000 years ago by the Chinese, but the ancient Egyptians also had quite intricate locks. They were often very large and usually consisted of a large bolt that was moved into a staple by a big key.

Who invented the safety pin?

People in the Middle Ages secured their clothing with pins of various types but it was not until 1849 that the modern safety pin was developed. It was invented by Walter Hunt of New York in order to repay someone 15 dollars. It took him just three hours to come up with the idea.

How does a Yale Lock work?

A Yale lock consists of a narrow cylinder revolving inside a larger, fixed cylinder. When the key is inserted into the keyhole the notches on the key push up a series of pins until they are all at the same level. This allows the key to turn, moving the inner cylinder and pulling back the bolt of the lock. The pins in each lock are different, so each has its own individual key.

Who invented the Yale Lock?

Linus Yale Jr. invented the cylinder lock now known as the Yale, in the 1860s. The big advantage of the Yale lock compared with other locks of the day was its superb engineering and the fact that it was smaller than any other key. As a result, Yale locks became popular the world over.

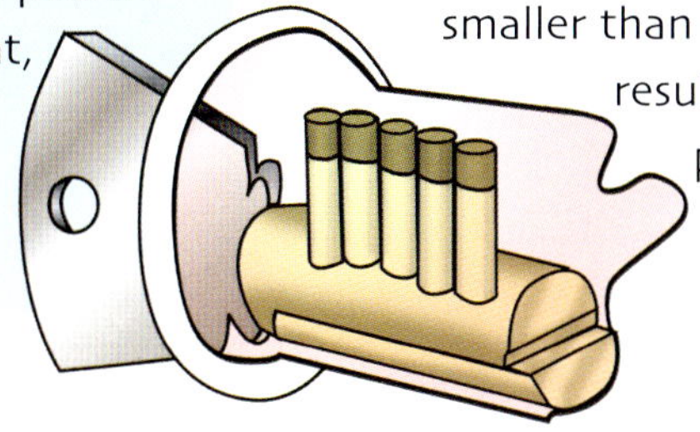

When was knitting invented?

Knitting appears to have originated in Arabia over 3,000 years ago. Some items knitted by nomadic tribesmen of that period exist to this day.

Who invented cat's-eyes?

Percy Shaw was driving late one night in 1934, when he thought of an idea that would revolutionise road travel. But his suggestion to put reflective studs on the roads did not appeal to the authorities. During the 'blackout' of the Second World War, car headlights had to be masked. This made it more difficult for drivers to see the road and 'cat's-eyes' were introduced on a large scale. Although the cat's-eyes were visible to the vehicle driver, they did not cast any light upward, so they could not be seen by enemy aircraft. This simple device is now used on roads all over the world.

Who invented the paperclip?

It was Johann Vaaler of Norway, who patented his invention in 1900.

Who invented the bowler hat?

In 1849, William Coke designed a hat that was so strong he could stamp on it without causing damage. It was made for him by hat-makers Thomas and William Bowler. The hat became very popular but instead of being called a 'coke' after its inventor, it attracted the name of 'bowler' from the people who made it.

Who invented the flush toilet?

The ancient Egyptians, Greeks and Roman all had toilets with flushing systems, but by the Middle Ages these had been forgotten. The first 'modern' flush toilet was designed by Sir John Harrington in 1589. It is thought only two were made, one for his own home and one for his godmother, Queen Elizabeth I.

Who invented Christmas cards?

In 1843, Sir Henry Cole decided to get in touch with all his friends at Christmas, but didn't have time to write to all of them. He asked artist John Horsley to design a card instead. After sending the cards to his friends, Cole found he had some left so he sold them in a London shop. Although people had sent cards before, it was not a common practice. Cole's cards changed all that and now billions are sent out each year all around the world.

Who invented Braille?

Louis Braille lost his sight when he was just a young boy. It was while working with leather, using his father's awl, that he came up with the idea of a raised writing system. He had used the awl to punch holes in leather and knew that if the awl did not go all the way through, it raised a prominent bump on the underside of the material. Blind people would be able to feel this bump and Braille turned his attention to developing a system of six raised dots that could be formed to represent letters. Braille's system was devised in 1824.

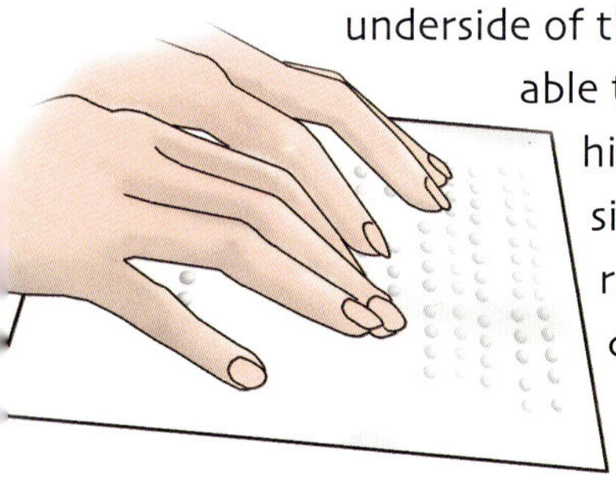

Who invented matches?

The first match was invented by accident. John Walker, a chemist, was mixing some chemicals with a stick and some of the mixture stuck to the wood. He tried to scrape it off on the stone floor and it burst into flames. The chemist realized the importance of his discovery and was soon making matches to sell in his shop. The first person to buy some was a solicitor, called Mr Hixon, who bought a box of Walker's matches on 7th April 1827.

Who invented the mackintosh?

In 1823 a Scottish chemist, Charles Mackintosh, discovered a way to dissolve rubber with a chemical called naptha. He sandwiched this rubber between two pieces of cloth to make a waterproof material. This material was too stiff to sew, but James Syme, a young medical student, found a new way to dissolve the rubber which made it softer and therefore easier to sew together to make raincoats.

When was the mirror invented?

There are several examples in existence of mirrors used by the ancient Greeks and Romans. The oldest dates from around 400 BC and consists of a highly polished, sheet of bronze. It was not until the 16th century, when the Venetians discovered how to make glass that gave the truest reflection, that glass mirrors came into fashion.

Who invented the Christmas cracker?

Tom Smith, a London sweet maker, was looking for a novelty for his sweets in 1846. A piece of wood cracked in his fire and this inspired him to invent the 'snap' that is used in crackers. The first crackers contained sweets.

Who made the first hover mower?

The Flymo Company produced the first hover mower, based on the principle of the hovercraft, in 1963.

Who invented the pillar box?

The idea of the British pillar box was conceived by Anthony Trollope. Although now best known as a writer, Trollope was once a postal official. In 1851, he was sent to the Channel Islands to inspect postal services. He found that people had to walk long distances to post letters, and suggested 'safe receptacles' be set up on the roadsides. Trollope had seen public mail boxes in France (the French adopted the idea from the Belgians, who first used mail boxes in 1849).

When was the first electric lawn mower developed?

The first patent for an electrically powered lawn mower was issued to Ransomes in 1926.

Who invented the lawn mower?

In 1805, Thomas Plucknett invented a two-wheeled machine with a circular blade, to cut grass and corn. The first mass-produced mowers were made in 1832, using a design invented by Edwin Budding two years earlier.

When was the motorized mower first produced?

The Ransomes company produced the first successful motorised lawn mower, in 1902 (although, experimental mowers had been designed in Germany and the USA several years earlier).

When was glue invented?

Glue dates back to ancient Egypt. The Egyptians would boil animal bones, horns and hides - a process that is still used for making some glues today.

Who invented the dishwasher?

For ten years, Mrs W A Cockran tried to persuade her husband to give her some money to develop a dishwashing machine she had invented, but he always refused. After his death, friends lent her some money and the machine was built in 1889. The dishwasher could reportedly wash, rinse and dry dishes of various shapes and sizes in just two minutes. The water was sprayed onto the dishes by a pump which was activated by turning a handle.

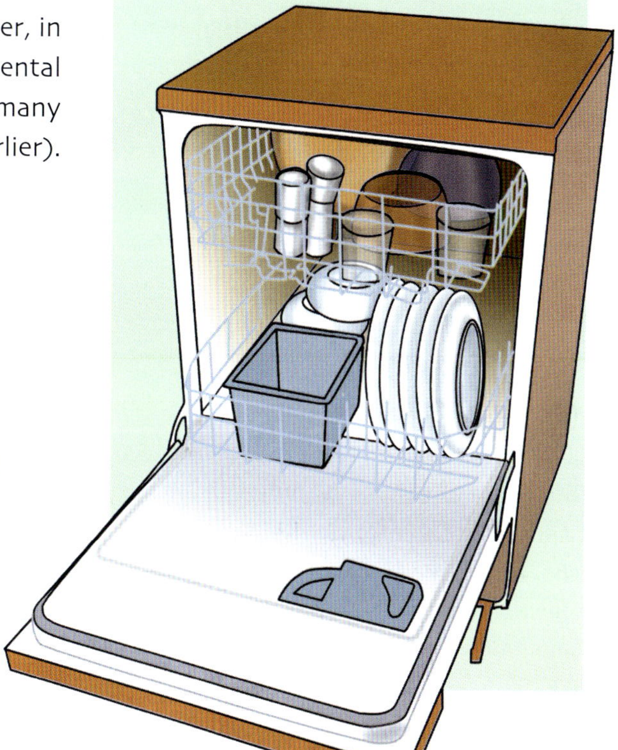

Who invented Worcestershire sauce?

Worcestershire sauce was created almost by accident. In 1835, Lord Sandys returned to Britain after a period of military service in India. He brought with him a recipe for a spicy Indian sauce and he asked chemists John W Lea and William Perrins to make some for him. They did so, but it tasted horrible, so they put the jars away. They forgot all about the sauce until they came across it in their cellar some time later. The pair tried it again and this time it was very tasty, having had time to mature. Lea and Perrins obtained permission to market the mixture and called it Worcestershire sauce, because they lived in Worcester.

The Wonders of Technology

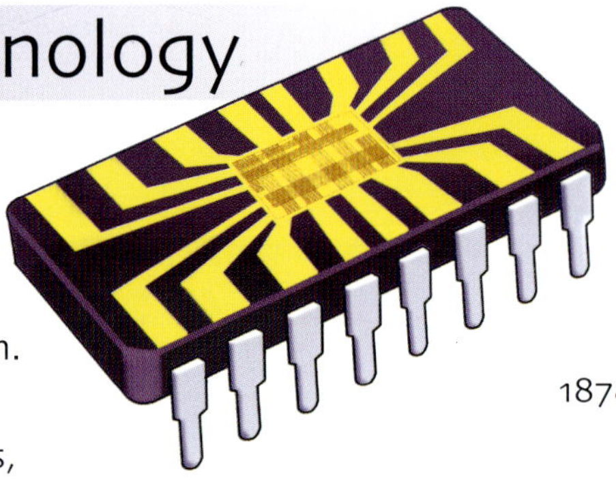

What is a silicon chip?

In 1953, Hardwick Johnson, of the Radio Corporation of America (RCA), built an electronic circuit on a tiny piece of germanium. By adding insulating layers on top of the germanium, it was possible to have transistors, capacitors and resistors all on the same chip - known as a silicon chip.

Which British town was the first to have electric street lighting?

The first proper tests of electric street lights were held in Westgate-on-Sea and London in 1878. By 1881 electric lights had been installed throughout the country.

How was electricity discovered?

The ancient Greeks discovered that amber rubbed with a dry cloth attracted small particles of the material. The word 'electricity' comes from the Greek Word 'elecktron', meaning amber.

Who invented television?

The Scottish electrical engineer John Logie Baird.

When did the first public television broadcast take place?

The first public television broadcast was made by the BBC on 30th September 1929.

Who made the first telephone call in Britain?

Alexander Graham Bell demonstrated the telephone in Britain on the Isle of Wight. The person to make the first call was Queen Victoria on 14th January 1878, to Sir Thomas Biddulph.

What was the first regular television service?

The world's first regular TV service was started by the BBC on 2nd November 1936. Transmissions ceased in 1939, two days before the outbreak of the Second World War. They re-started on 7th June 1946, the eve of the Victory parades.

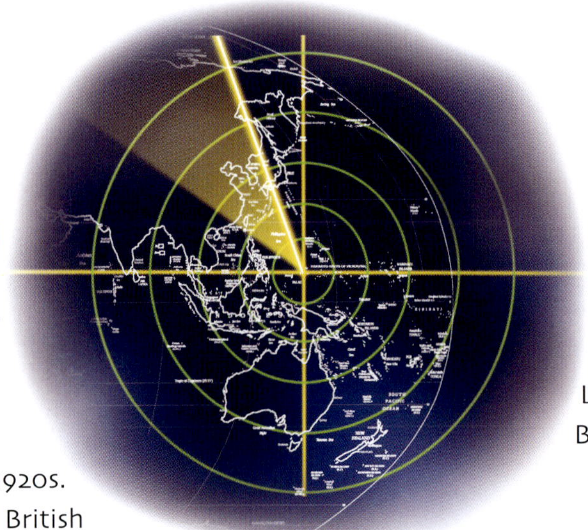

Who invented radar?

The basic principle of radar (the reflection of short radio waves) was discovered in the 1920s. But it wasn't until British scientist Robert Watson-Watt began experimenting with radio waves that this method (of detecting an object's position and speed), became a possibility. The world's first radar station opened in Britain in 1935. The word 'radar' is short for 'Radio Detecting and Ranging'.

Who was the first person to appear on television?

The first person to have his image transmitted by television was William Taynton, a 15-year-old London office boy, on 2nd October 1925. John Logie Baird had just succeeded in transmitting a picture of a ventriloquist's dummy from one room to another and wanted a live subject. Taynton happened to be the first person he saw as he rushed out to the street to find someone. But the boy was so frightened by all the lights and strange machinery that Baird had to give him some pocket money before he would submit to the experiment.

Who invented the radio?

As a child, Guglielmo Marconi of Italy was fascinated by electricity. At the age of 20, he achieved his first radio transmission - sending the three dots of Morse code letter S from one end of his attic to the other. Shortly after, he and his brother, Alfonso, were sending signals over longer distances. The Italian government were not interested in his work so Marconi went to England, where the British Post Office gave him support. On 12th December 1901, Marconi succeeded in beaming Morse code signals across the Atlantic.

Who was the first to transmit speech by radio?

The first person to transmit speech by radio was R A Fessenden of the University of Pittsburgh in the USA. On Christmas Eve 1906, he transmitted speech and music over several hundred kilometres - the first true radio broadcast.

What was the first entertainment broadcast?

On 12th June 1920, the Marconi Company broadcasted a recital by the opera singer Dame Nellie Melba. All further broadcasts for entertainment purposes were immediately banned, as officials thought them too trivial for such an important means of communication. In 1921, the ban was relaxed and half an hour of speech and music broadcasting was permitted each week.

Who had the first electric traffic lights?

The first electrically operated traffic lights were installed at a busy crossroad in Ohio, USA, on 5th August 1914. Drivers were warned the lights were about to change by means of a loud buzzer. The first electrically operated lights in Britain came into service in London in 1926.

Where were traffic lights first used?

In the late 19th century, British politicians had trouble turning their carriages safely into the Palace of Westminster. In response, the Metropolitan Commissioner of Police, Richard Mayne, organised the introduction of a traffic control system of red and green gas-powered lights. They came into operation on 10th December, 1868. The lights were controlled by a lever at the base but its operation was unreliable. Just a few weeks after the control's installation, a police officer was injured when the apparatus exploded. The lights were unpopular and remained in service for only a few years.

What was the first computer?

Over the centuries, many machines and devices have been invented to help Man with complicated calculations. The first computer in the modern sense was the 'Analytical Engine' invented by Charles Baggage in 1834. Unfortunately, it was too difficult for Victorian engineers to make and was not built until the 1990s, by which time computers were commonplace.

What is binary?

The system of counting we use every day is based on the number ten. Binary works on the number two. There are just two digits, 1 and 0. This makes the system ideal for computers because the two digits can be represented by an electrical signal being switched off for one digit and on for the other.

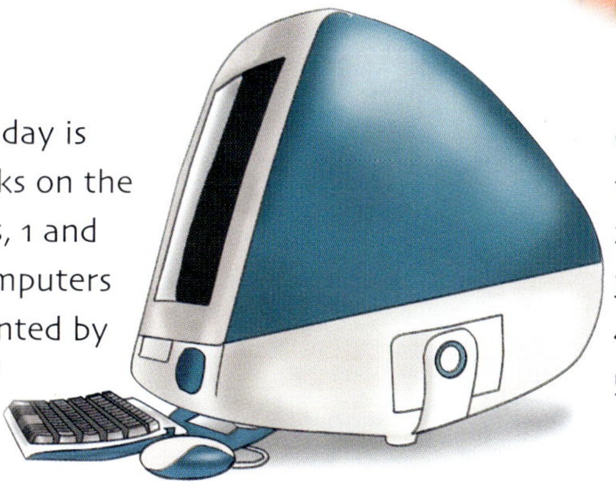

0	0	6	110	12	1100
1	1	7	111	13	1101
2	10	8	1000	14	1110
3	11	9	1001	15	1111
4	100	10	1010	16	10000
5	101	11	1011		

The First ...

When was food first cooked?

Man first discovered cooking during the Stone Age, after learning to make fire. A caveman probably dropped a piece of meat onto a fire by accident and then found that it smelled (and tasted) rather good.

Where is the world's first iron bridge?

The world's first iron bridge spans a gorge through which the River Severn flows near Coalbrookdale in Shropshire. Built in 1779 by Abraham Darby, it remains a unique monument to the industrial revolution. It was such a remarkable structure that a small township about half a mile from Coalbrookdale was named Ironbridge. Much of the area is now a vast open-air museum.

Who was the first person to be buried in St Paul's Cathedral?

St Paul's Cathedral in London was finished in 1710. Its designer, Sir Christopher Wren, died in 1723 at the age of 90. He was the first person to be buried there.

Who was the first ever English Pope?

So far only one Englishman has been Pope. He was Nicholas Breakspear, who was elected with the name Pope Adrian IV, in December 1154.

Who was the first Prince of Wales?

In 1301, King Edward I of England invested his eldest son, Edward, as the Prince of Wales. King Edward's main purpose in creating this title was probably to placate the Welsh people after his wars of conquest. Since then, the title has been conferred upon the male heir apparent of the sovereign.

Which was the first stagecoach to cross America?

John Butterfield's Overland Mail Company which carried mail across the USA during the 1850-60s.

When was the top hat first worn?

James Hetherington wore the first top hat in London on 5th January 1797. He was promptly arrested because his new headgear caused quite a disturbance: a huge crowd gathered round him, in which many people started to panic and even faint!

Why are flags sometimes flown at half mast?

Flags are flown at half mast as a sign of mourning and respect for someone who has recently died.

When was a flag first flown at half mast?

In 1626 James Hall, leader of an expedition to find the North-west Passage, was killed by a group of Inuit. The flag on board his ship, the Hartsease, was lowered to half mast as a mark of respect.

Who was the first to run a mile in under four minutes?

In 1954 an English doctor, Roger Bannister, ran a mile in just 3 minutes 59.4 seconds. He was the first known man to break the four minute barrier.

Who used the first envelope?

In 1696 Sir James Ogilvie sent a letter to Sir William Turnbull and put it into an envelope measuring 11 centimetres (4 1/4 in) by 8 centimetres (3 in). But envelopes did not come into general use until the launch of the penny post in 1840, for they were charged as an extra sheet.

Who was the first person to wear roller skates?

In 1760 Joseph Merlin entered a masquerade party in London, on roller skates. Playing a violin, he glided across the room. Unfortunately, he could not stop or change direction and smashed into a large mirror. The mirror was broken, his violin was smashed and he was badly hurt!

Who was the first person to write a detective story?

'The Murders in the Rue Morgue' (published by Graham's Magazine, Philadelphia in 1841) is considered the world's first detective story. It was written by Edgar Allan Poe.

When were houses first given numbers?

The first time houses were numbered was in 1463, on the Pont Notre-Dame in Paris.

Who was the first magician?

The first person to entertain with 'magic' is unknown. The first of whom there is any definite record is Dedi, who performed before King Cheops of Egypt over 5,000 years ago. His amazing feats are detailed in an ancient papyrus which is kept in a Berlin museum.

When were elastic bands first used?

The first elastic bands were made by Perry and Company of London in 1845, under a patent issued to the company on 17th March of that year.

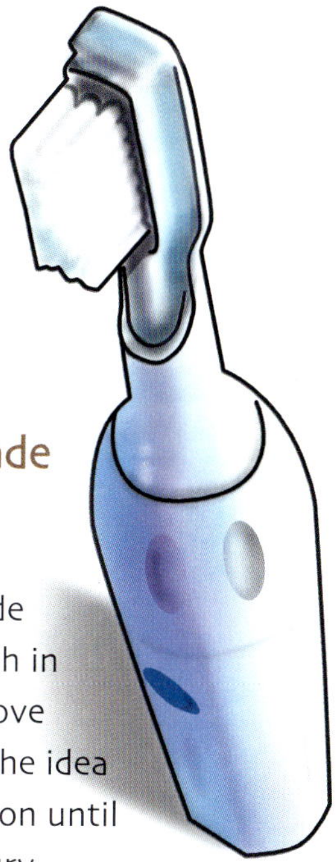

Who made the first toothbrush?

William Addis made the first toothbrush in 1780. It did not prove very popular and the idea didn't really catch on until the late 19th century.

When was the first multi-storey car park opened?

The City & Suburban Electric Carriage Company of London opened their multi-storey car park in May 1901. It had seven storeys and a lift to carry vehicles to the top.

Which country was the first to issue driving licences?

France was the first country to issue driving licences, in 1893. In the same year, France also became the first country to insist upon a driving test for all motorists.

When did white lines first appear on British roads?

Before white lines were painted down the centre of British roads, drivers generally kept to the left, but they often strayed. Kent County Alderman Amos suggested using white lines to separate the two traffic flows on some dangerous roads in Kent in 1914. Gradually, the idea spread through the nation.

Which was the first newspaper?

Public newspapers as we know them today are a relatively modern development, although attempts to inform the public date back to ancient Rome. Possibly the first 'newspaper' was the acta diurna (daily acts) which were reports of important events designed to inform the people of Rome.

What was the first comic?

The first comic was Comic Cuts, published on 17th May 1890. The first editions did not contain strips as we know them today and had more words than pictures. The first comic strip was published in Comic Cuts on 7th June 1890. Comic Cuts was written for adults and it was not for another 30 years that the first comic for children, The Rainbow, was published.

What was the first comic strip in a newspaper?

The first comic strip to appear in a newspaper was The Yellow Kid, which appeared in a colour supplement of The New York Journal on 24th October 1897.

What was the first credit card?

When people buy things today they often use a credit card. They do not have to pay in cash as the amount of the transaction is charged direct to their bank account or they pay part or all of the outstanding bill at the end of the month. Shortly after the First World War, petrol companies in the USA began to issue such cards which allowed people to get petrol without having to pay for it at the time. After the Second World War, this idea spread to hotels and department stores, which began issuing their own cards. The first credit card to cover all types of purchases was Diners Club, which dates back to the early 1950s.

Who was the first man on the moon?

Neil Armstrong, the American astronaut stepped down from the lunar module 'Eagle' on 20th July 1969, becoming the first human to set foot on the moon.

What were the first words spoken on the moon?

"That's one small step for Man, one giant leap for mankind," uttered Neil Armstrong as he landed on the moon in 1969.

When was a mechanical hare first used in dog racing?

A mechanical hare was first used to entice greyhounds to race in London, on 6th October 1876. The hare was drawn along a straight, 3,645 metre (3,986 yd) track by a rope wound around a windlass. In 1895, a mechanical hare was tried in Ireland but did not prove popular, and it was not until 1923 in the USA that the idea really caught on.

What was the first aeroplane to have a toilet?

The Russian passenger plane Russky Vitiaz, first flown in May 1913, was the first aircraft with a toilet on board.

What was the first railway train to have a toilet?

In 1859, George Pullman installed a toilet at each end of a sleeping car used on the Chicago & Alton railroad.

Precious Stones and Metals

What are the crown jewels?

The crown jewels are a collection of jewellery and regalia that symbolises the authority of the British monarchy. The jewels are sometimes worn by the monarch on state occasions. Among the most important items are the Imperial State Crown, the Royal Sceptre (which holds the largest cut diamond in the world) and the Sword of State.

Who tried to steal the crown jewels?

In 1671, Captain Thomas Blood pretended to fall in love with the jewel-keeper's daughter to get himself into the Tower of London. He pretended to be a clergyman and the jewel keeper believed him. Blood knocked the man on the head and stole some crowns. He did not get very far though, before he was stopped by an off-duty soldier. Much to everyone's surprise the King, Charles II, pardoned Blood and even awarded him a special pension for his daring deed!

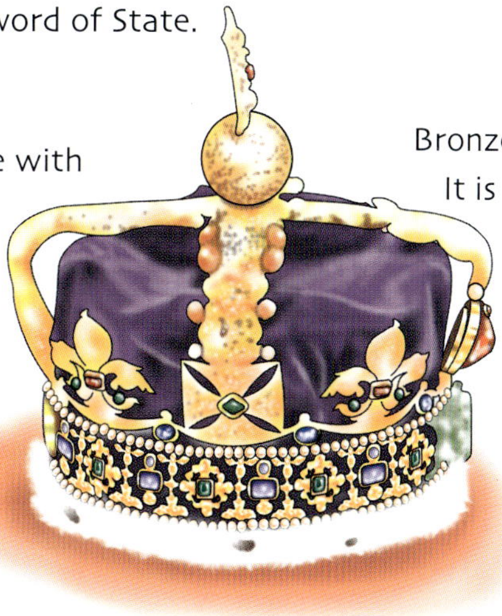

What is bronze?

Bronze is an alloy of copper and tin. It is one of the oldest metal alloys known to Man and has been used since about 5000 BC. Bronze is extremely strong and does not rust or corrode.

What is an alloy?

An alloy is a blend of metal with one or more other metals. Most are made by melting one metal and then adding the others. The alloy is usually much harder or stronger than any of the metals used to make it.

Where are the crown jewels kept?

In the Tower of London. In 1994, they were moved to a special display centre, in the former Waterloo Barracks.

What is black diamond?

There are dark diamonds that are, sometimes, called 'black' but the term is more often used to describe coal.

Why are diamonds valuable?

The value of a precious stone or metal is determined by its appearance and rarity. For centuries, diamonds have been regarded as the most brilliant of precious stones, for when cut they are particularly attractive in the way they reflect light. At one time, diamonds were extremely rare and were used more as symbols of power than as jewellery. This was so until the 15th century, when ladies of the royal court of France started a fashion for diamond jewellery. There has been a demand ever since!

For how much are the crown jewels insured?

Because they are of such great historical significance and immense importance to the country, the crown jewels are not insured. It is estimated that they are worth over £ 100 million, so great care is taken to ensure that they are very well protected.

What unit is used for weighing gold?

Gold, diamonds and other precious stones are weighed in carats. The name comes from the seeds of the locust bean, which were once used to weigh precious stones.

Which metal is liquid?

At normal temperature, just one metal is in liquid state - mercury. It has to be at 40°C (120°F) to become a solid.

Who would use a crampon?

A crampon is a type of metal plate with spikes on it. Mountaineers attach crampons to their boots to give them a better grip in snow and ice.

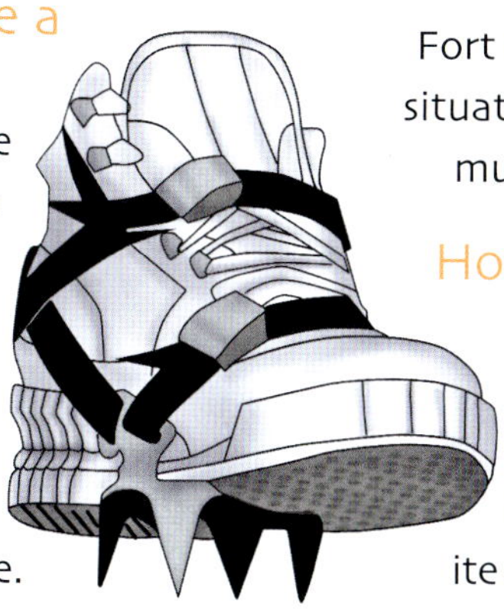

What is Fort Knox?

Fort Knox is the USA's gold depository, situated in Hardin, Kentucky. It contains much of the nation's gold reserves.

How much gold is in Fort Knox?

The actual amount of gold stored in Fort Knox is a closely guarded secret. The depository - a bomb-proof building made of concrete, steel and granite and equipped with numerous security devices - is guarded day and night.

Faiths and Beliefs

Who was Buddha?

Gautam of Siddhartha (circa 563-483 BC) was brought up in India, in luxury. When he was 29, he gave up his wealth to seek the true meaning of life. Six years later, he found enlightenment, hence the name Buddha, meaning 'the enlightened one'. He then devoted the rest of his life to teaching others how to find enlightenment and Buddhism is now one of the great world religions.

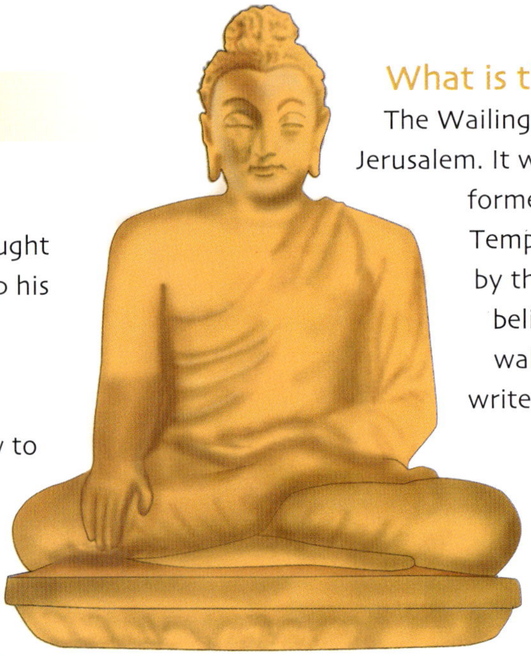

What is the 'Wailing' Wall?

The Wailing Wall is a sacred place in Jerusalem. It was built in AD 70 on the former site of King Solomon's Temple, which was destroyed by the Romans. Many people believe prayers given at the wall will be answered. They write the prayers on pieces of paper and place them in cracks in the wall.

What is Halloween?

The word 'Halloween' is an abbreviation of 'All Hallows Evening', the evening before All Saints Day (the word 'hallows' meaning saints). It also has an association with witches, but this goes back to pagan times. The 31st October used to be the last day of the year and was celebrated in the same way that we still celebrate New Year's Eve. It was originally a festival of fire, the dead and the forces of evil. The fire part of the celebrations has now moved to 5th November - Bonfire Night. It was believed that on Halloween the dead rose from the grave and witches roamed the skies on their broomsticks. The ancient celebrations were treated with fear and suspicion, but today Halloween is an occasion to dress up and have fun.

What are the seven deadly sins?

The seven deadly sins are pride, avarice, envy, lust, sloth, gluttony and anger.

Why is Mecca important to Muslims?

Mohammed, founder of the Muslim religion, Islam, was born in Mecca around AD 570. It is the Holy city of Islam. Muslims must face towards it when they pray and visit Mecca at least once in their lifetime.

Why do we have eggs at Easter?

Easter occurs at springtime, which is the start of the growing season. Ancient people used eggs as a symbol of new births, so they became associated with spring. The early Christians adopted this idea and for them eggs represented the resurrection of Jesus Christ. It became common practice to paint eggs and give them to family and friends at Easter.

When were chocolate Easter eggs first made?

Chocolate Easter eggs were first made at the end of the 19th century. Today, in the British Isles alone, over 80 million chocolate eggs are bought every year.

What was the Holy Grail?

The Holy Grail was the legendary cup from which Jesus drank at the Last Supper. Some tales of King Arthur tell of his knights' search for the Grail.

What is Shinto?

Shinto is an ancient religion of Japan, and the word 'Shinto' means 'The Way of the Gods'. The Gods of Shinto are the forces of nature and, as there were so many of them, it is also known as 'the religion of the million gods'.

Why are Church lecterns in the form of an eagle ?

In many churches, the Bible is placed upon a reading stand called a lectern. Very often this is made of carved wood or brass to represent an eagle with outstretched wings. The eagle is a symbol of Jesus Christ's return to life after his death. It has been a religious symbol for a very long time, but lecterns shaped as eagles were unknown before the 13th century.

Food

What is Haggis?

Haggis is a popular Scottish dish made from the finely chopped heart, liver and lungs of a sheep, mixed with onion, oatmeal, herbs and seasoning. These ingredients are put together in the lining of a sheep's stomach and boiled for several hours. The recipe dates back to, at least, the Middle Ages.

What is a bouquet garni?

A bouquet garni is a collection of different herbs (usually tied together) used in cooking. The basic bouquet garni contains a bay leaf and sprigs of thyme and parsley. Marjoram is also a popular herb, while many cooks wrap celery around the herbs before tying them together. Instead of being tied, the herbs can also be placed loosely in a muslin bag. This makes the bouquet easier to find when the cook wants to remove it.

When was tea first brought to Europe?

Tea was introduced to Europe by the East India Company in 1609. Doctors recommended tea as a cure for many ills and some people, reportedly, drank up to 100 cups a day.

When were baked beans invented?

Baked beans have been a popular dish since at least the early 19th century. Back then, the making of baked beans in the USA was a weekly affair that involved the whole family. In 1875, the fishermen of Maine wanted to enjoy their beans while away at sea, so a local company, Burnham & Morrill, began canning baked beans.

What is Bombay Duck?

Bombay Duck is a dish of dried, salted fish. The type of fish used is the bummalo, which is rather like salmon. Bombay, India, is one of the main trading centres for this fish - hence 'Bombay' in the name - but where the 'Duck' name comes from is unclear. Bombay Duck is usually eaten as a relish with curries and similar dishes.

Who invented potato crisps?

In 1853, an American Indian chief, George Crum, was working at a hotel in Florida. A customer requested some fried potatoes but wanted them very thinly cut. They were fried, but to a frazzle. Luckily, the customer liked them. Others began asking for the same and the great potato crisp was born.

What is a calorie?

We often hear of calorie-controlled diets, but what exactly is a calorie? It is a unit of heat defined as the amount of energy needed to raise the temperature of a gram of water through one degree centigrade. It is often used to measure the energy value of foods.

When was the pop-up toaster introduced?

The General Electric Company sold the first electric toasters in 1927, in New York. They toasted only one side of the bread, so each slice had to be turned around by hand to toast the other side. The first pop-up toaster, toasting the bread on both sides at once, and releasing the bread after a given time, was invented by Charles Strite of Minnesota.

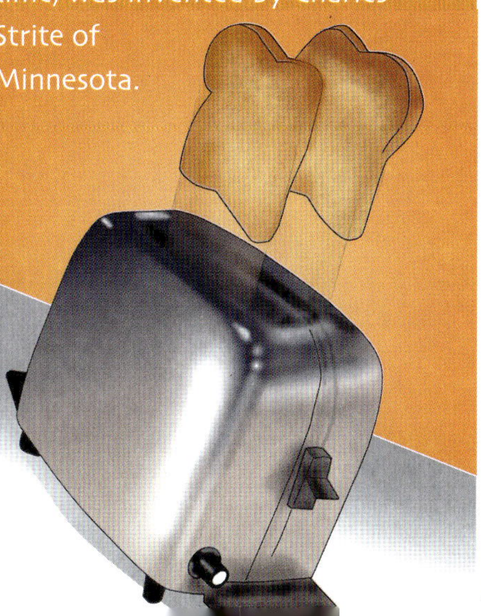

How did the chef's hat get its shape?

According to tradition, the chef's hat was originally designed by the great Italian Renaissance painter Leonardo da Vinci (1452-1519). As well as being a painter, sculptor, architect and engineer, he was also a good cook! The hat was then redesigned by Antonin Careme in the late 18th century. In the 19th century, Alexis Soyer starched the pleats so the hat would stay upright and give the chef's head some ventilation.

How is chewing gum made?

A man called a 'chicler' is the first person involved in making chewing gum. It is his job to climb the capodilla tree, where he makes deep gashes in the trunk. The sap, or chicle, leaks from the tree and into a pot on the ground. The chicle is then boiled and poured into moulds to solidify. It is sent to a factory where it is chopped up and boiled again to ensure all the impurities are removed. Vegetable oil is added to soften the chicle, as well as sugar, syrup and flavourings. The blended gum is now formed into a long slab which is cut into sticks before being wrapped.

What is tapioca?

Tapioca - delicious when made into a dessert - originates from the poisonous roots of the cassava plant, which grows in tropical regions. When the starchy substance inside the roots is heated, the poison evaporates. The heat also transforms the tapioca into clear pellets, which is how it appears when bought in shops. When cooked in milk, the tapioca softens and swells. In appearance, it resembles frogspawn - the nickname given to it by many British children.

What was the first breakfast cereal?

Henry D Perky, an American, suffered with a bad stomach. One day he saw a man eating whole boiled wheat with milk for breakfast. This seemed the ideal solution to his stomach problems, so in 1893 Perky invented shredded wheat. Two years on, he began producing the cereal on a large scale.

Where does nutmeg come from?

A nutmeg is the hard kernel of an East Indian evergreen. To preserve the flavour, the nutmegs are exported whole and grated only when required to flavour foods.

What is yoghurt?

Yoghurt is milk which has been impregnated with live bacteria. Plain yoghurt can be eaten as is, or used in a wide variety of cooking. Most yoghurt bought in shops is flavoured with fruit or other foods and is eaten on its own or poured over desserts.

What are raisins?

Raisins are dried grapes which are grown in California, the Mediterranean and Australia. Originally, the grapes were dried in the sun, but now most are dried in specially heated buildings. At one time the word 'raisin' was also used to describe what are now known as currants and sultanas, both of which are also made from dried grapes.

What is Sauerkraut?

Cabbage pickled in brine. Originating from Germany, it is made by packing alternate layers of cabbage and salt in a large barrel. When it has fermented slightly, it is then bottled or canned.

When was wine first made?

The history of wine can be traced back to 1500 BC. It is referred to in the Old Testament of the Bible and the ancient Assyrians and Egyptians were great wine-makers.

How did the 'hot dog' get its name?

Near the end of the 19th century, Harry Stevens sold Frankfurter sausages at baseball stadiums in the USA. Because the sausages were hot, he put them in bread rolls. A cartoonist happened to draw Harry's stall but because he could not spell dachshund (Harry's nickname for the sausages), he called them hot dogs - and the name has remained ever since.

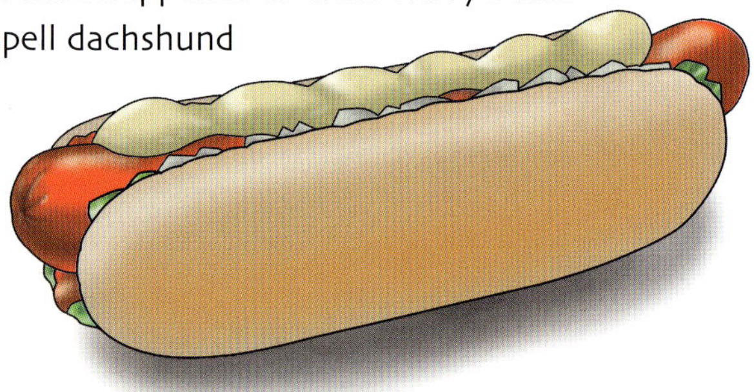

What is caviar?

Caviar is the roe (eggs) of the sturgeon fish to which salt has been added. It has a very strong flavour and is regarded as a great delicacy.

What is saffron?

A yellow substance used for colouring and flavouring food. It is made from the stigmas of a particular type of crocus, and is very expensive because it takes over 4,000 stigmas to produce just one ounce.

Which country produces the most types of cheese?

There are about 450 named cheeses made around the world. Over half, some 240, are made in France.

Where do hamburgers come from?

Although the hamburger is now associated mainly with the USA, it came originally from Russia. In medieval times, a favourite Russian food was shredded raw meat seasoned with salt, pepper and onion juice. German sailors visiting the Baltic ports, liked the meat and took the recipe back to the port of Hamburg in Germany - hence, the name 'hamburger'. Unable to face the thought of eating the meat raw, the Germans usually grilled it. In the 19th century, German immigrants took the recipe with them to America. In 1900, Louis Larsen served the dish between two slices of bread to make it easier to eat and the American hamburger was born.

Did the Romans eat bread?

Bread was in existence long before Roman times. It has been the staple food of people all over the world. The Romans certainly ate bread and there were almost 260 bakers in Rome alone, around 100 BC. At a later date, the Roman emperor Trajan even founded a school for bakers.

Where does mace come from?

Mace is a spice widely used in cooking. It is in fact, the outer covering of the nutmeg which has been dried in the sun.

Why is a chicken wishbone used for wishing?

There are several ancient ways of telling fortunes by using bones. Pulling a wishbone and making a wish has developed from these. It is said that the person who gets the larger part of the wishbone when it is broken will have his or her wish granted.

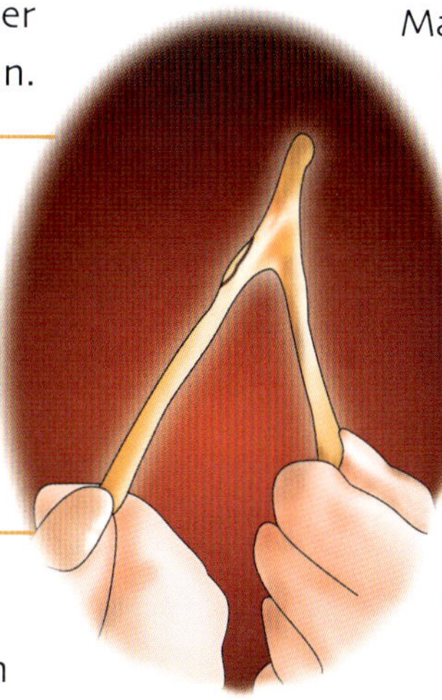

What is marzipan?

Marzipan is a paste that is used to cover cakes, or is made into sweets. It is a mixture of sugar and almonds (in fact, it is often called 'almond paste').

What is an ugli?

An ugli is a fruit. It is a cross between a grapefruit, a tangerine and an orange.

What are Scotch eggs?

Scotch eggs are hard-boiled eggs that have been covered with sausage meat, then coated with breadcrumbs and fried.

Who invented fish fingers?

The fish finger was invented by the Bird's Eye food company in 1955. By 1994, Bird's Eye had sold some 14 billion!

Who put the hole in a ring doughnut?

It is said this innovation was the idea of a boy called Hanson Gregory, in 1847. He enjoyed his mother's doughnuts but they were always doughy in the centre. One day, he suggested she cut out the middle before frying them. The resulting doughnuts were perfect. And so, the ring doughnut was born!

Trees and Plants

Why do trees shed their leaves?

As the days become shorter, the food-making process of leaves slows down and the leaves of deciduous trees wither and fall. This prevents the tree from losing moisture through the leaves' pores, which would be harmful during the winter months.

How did the dandelion get its name?

The name 'dandelion' probably originated in Norman times. People thought the leaves resembled lions' teeth, so the plant was called 'dent de lion' (lion's tooth). Over time 'dent de lion' gradually became 'dandelion'.

Where does castor oil come from?

Castor oil is obtained from the seeds of a plant which is sometimes called Palma Christi, but is better known as the castor oil plant. This plant is actually a tall shrub that grows to about 2 metres in height.

What do leaves do?

The leaf takes water and minerals absorbed from the soil by the tree's roots, which are carried up to the leaf by tubes. These nutrients combine with carbon dioxide from the air. With the aid of energy from sunlight, it turns these substances into sugar, which is food for the tree.

What is an oak apple?

Oak apples are swellings caused by the gall wasp, which lays its eggs on the oak tree. When the eggs have hatched the grubs eat their way through the spongy flesh of the apple.

How is dew formed?

After a warm day, the temperature drops at night and the air and the water vapour in it become chilled. The water vapour becomes heavy and settles on the cooled leaves of plants.

Why do cactus plants have spines?

As the cactus lives in dry regions, it has to cope with lack of water. To absorb water quickly, the plant's roots remain near the surface of the ground; water is stored in its spongy stem.
The prickly spines reduce water loss and have one other advantage - a thirsty animal is unlikely to bite into the spiny cactus to quench its thirst!

How is rubber made?

Rubber is made from latex, a milky fluid obtained from the rubber (Hevea) tree. A groove is cut into the bark and the latex oozes into a cup attached to the tree. The latex is then mixed with an acid, which causes it to coagulate so that it can be pressed into sheet form. It is then crushed and mixed with various chemicals in a process called vulcanisation, which was discovered by Charles Goodyear in 1839. The rubber is then made into the many rubber products that we use today.

Where do cashew nuts come from?

Cashew nuts grow on a small evergreen tree found in Central and South America. The shells contain a poisonous substance, which is removed by roasting. Sometimes this poisonous oil is extracted and can be used to protect timber from termites.

Where does cork come from?

Cork is the outer layers of a type of oak tree found in Spain and Portugal.

What is camomile?

Camomile is a plant, the flowers of which look like daisies. Because it has such a pleasant scent, it was often used in the Middle Ages to spread on the floors of houses to make them smell fresh. When infused with hot water, camomile makes a pleasant drink reputed to ease indigestion and promote relaxation.

Insects

How do grasshoppers hear?

With their stomachs! They do not have ears and rely upon a special hearing organ in their middle section.

Why does a glow-worm glow?

The insects we call glow-worms may be either luminous, wingless beetles or fireflies. On the underside of the glow-worm most familiar in Europe, is a layer of oily tissue that, by chemical action, produces a glow. A second layer of tissue acts as a reflector and the outer transparent skin serves as a lens. Light is produced when the female wishes to attract a mate. With its specially large eyes, the male is able to see the glow and is attracted to it.

Which food and fabric colouring was made from crushed insects?

The red colouring cochineal was once made from the crushed bodies of a beetle found in Central America. Nowadays it is made from synthetic dyes for clothing and vegetable dyes for food colouring.

How does a fly walk on the ceiling?

Highly magnified pictures of a housefly's foot show that it is composed of two fleshy pads. On these pads are modified hairs which are, in fact, tubes with a mushroom shaped sucker at the ends. From these suckers there is a secretion which is slightly sticky and which enables the fly to stick to any surface. To remove itself from the surface, the fly raises its foot obliquely so that each row of hair is removed separately.

Do moths eat clothes?

There are six species of moth that damage clothes, carpets and upholstery. But it is not the moth itself that does the damage, it's the moth's larvae. Moths lay eggs on the material and when the larvae hatch they start munching!

How strong is an ant?

An ant is so strong, it can lift fifty times its own weight.

How many legs do centipedes and millipedes have?

Centipedes and millipedes are segmented worm-like creatures which have a pair of legs growing from each segment. The word 'centipede' means 'hundred footed' and 'millipede' means 'thousand footed'. Centipedes may have from 28 to over a hundred legs, but millipedes have nowhere near a thousand legs as their name suggests.

Why is the death's head hawk moth so called?

The death's head hawk moth, found in Europe, acquired its name because the markings on its thorax often look like a human skull.

What are silverfish?

Silverfish are scaly, wingless insects commonly found in homes, particularly in moist areas or where there is food. They are about 1.7 centimetres (1/2 in) long, covered in silver scales and dart away at great speed when disturbed. They are harmless and, although they eat food scraps, they seldom actually spoil food.

Where do flies go in winter?

Flies hibernate during the winter months, but many of them die with the onset of cold weather. In order to hatch, the egg of a fly has to be between 24°C (76°F) and 35°C (95°F) - another reason why so few flies are seen in winter.

Where does a bee keep its sting?

A bee's sting is at the tip of its abdomen. It consists of a shaft of two barbed lancets running on 'rails' on the pointed stylet. The lancets move forward alternately and penetrate deep into the victim. Poison is then pumped down the central canal and into the wound.

How did the ladybird get its name?

In the Middle Ages this insect was dedicated to the Virgin Mary. It became known as the 'Beetle of Our Lady', which over time was shortened to 'ladybird'.

Are ladybirds useful?

Ladybirds are certainly useful to gardeners because they feed on aphids (tiny insects), which can damage plants. Some market gardeners buy ladybirds for their plants, to control pests without using harmful chemicals.

How many types of ladybirds are there?

There are some 3,000 species of ladybirds around the world.

Are ladybirds known by any other names?

Yes, in the USA the bright beetles are called ladybugs.

What is a ladybird's favourite colour?

Many aphids that ladybirds eat tend to be found on yellow flowers. Wear a yellow T-shirt in summer and you may end up covered with ladybirds!

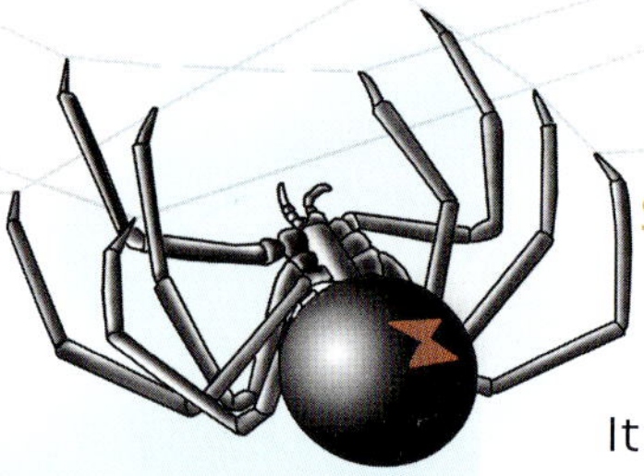

Why is the black widow spider so called?

The black widow is a poisonous spider found in North America. It is all black except for a red, hour-glass-shaped mark on its underside. It is called the black widow because the female often eats her mate!

How strong is spiders' silk?

It is thought the silk spun by spiders to make webs is stronger than steel. At one time the US military were planning to make a bullet-proof jacket made of spiders' silk.

What is the biggest beetle?

The biggest beetle in the world is the goliath beetle, which lives in Africa. It can measure up to 11.4 cms (4.5 in) long and weigh up to 100 grams (3.5 oz).

Why is the deathwatch beetle so called?

This beetle acquired its strange name because people once believed the clicking sound it makes is a sign of impending death. The beetle burrows through wood, and the sound is actually the female beetle tapping its head against the tunnel walls to attract a mate.

Birds and Animals

How do you determine the age of a tortoise?

A tortoise's shell consists of plates, which are covered with horny shields. On these shields there are rings. The number of rings determines the creature's age in years. This system only works with young tortoises, for as they get older the shields are worn smooth.

Who was killed by a tortoise?

According to comic legend the Greek poet Aeschylus was killed by a tortoise. Aeschylus was bald, and it is said that an eagle mistook his head for a stone. It dropped the tortoise it was carrying, hoping that the 'stone' would break the shell. Unfortunately it killed the poet instead!

What is an aardvark?

The aardvark is about the size of a pig and has very long ears. It lives in central and southern Africa and its name, from the Boer language, means 'earth pig'.

How fast can a mole dig?

A mole can dig a tunnel two metres long in just 12 minutes. It is not unusual for a mole to dig a tunnel of 100 metres (329 ft) in length in just one night.

What is a duck-billed platypus?

This strange river creature lives in Australia and Tasmania. It has a soft duck-like bill, webbed feet and a broad tail. It is one of only two mammals that lay eggs, the other being the spiny anteater.

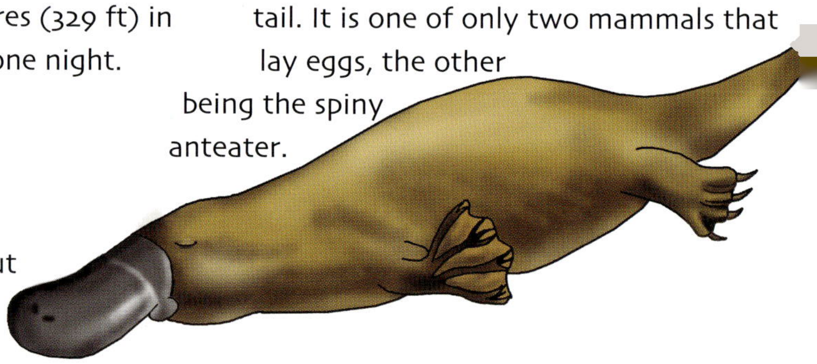

Why does a hippopotamus live in water?

The water helps to support the immense weight of the hippopotamus. Life could be quite uncomfortable for the animal if it had to live on land. They do, however, come out of the water quite a lot, particularly at night.

Where would you find a dingo in the wild?

A dingo is the wild dog of Australia. Its origin is uncertain, but some people believe that the Aborigines brought it from Asia.

Which is the tallest dog?

The tallest dogs are great danes, which can be up to 81 centimetres (32 in) high at the shoulder. Great danes were originally bred in Germany some 400 years ago, for hunting wild boar.

Which is the smallest breed of dog?

The chihuahua can weigh as little as 0.5 kilograms (1.1 lb). It is named after a Mexican mining town. Other dogs of similar size are the toy poodle and the Yorkshire terrier. In fact, the smallest dog on record was a Yorkshire terrier weighing 113 grams (4 oz).

Are pigs dirty animals?

No, pigs like to live in clean conditions. They do, however, wallow in mud in hot weather - the mud helps to keep them cool.

Which dog does not bark?

The basenji, which comes from Africa, does not bark.

Which is the smallest mammal?

Not a great deal is known about the Savi's white-toothed pygmy shrew, which lives in Southern Europe and Africa. It is about 4 centimetres (1.5 in) long, has a tail of 2 centimetres (3/4 in) and weighs around 2 grams (0.07 oz) which makes it the smallest non-flying mammal known to Man.

Why do dogs turn around before lying down?

When dogs were wild, they would turn round and round to trample down the grass to make a comfortable bed upon which to sleep. Even though dogs have now been domesticated for thousands of years and have no need to do this, the habit remains.

What is an echidna?

An echidna is a spiny, egg-laying, burrowing animal that lives in Australia and New Guinea. It is a type of anteater and looks like a hedgehog. When attacked, it rolls itself up into a ball.

What is a burro?

It is a small domesticated ass that is used as a pack animal and is found mainly in Mexico.

How do you determine a horse's age?

By looking at its teeth. When a horse is very young it has only incisors. At the age of four, its milk teeth should have been replaced by permanent teeth. By looking at the growth and shape of the permanent teeth, an expert can estimate the horse's age up to about nine years. At about ten years of age a groove (called Galvayne's groove) appears on the rear incisors. Slowly the groove increases in length, and by the time the horse is 15, it is half the length of the tooth. When the horse is between 25 and 30, Galvayne's groove gradually disappears.

Why do dogs bury bones?

When dogs lived in the wild, they were always under threat of attack by other dogs while eating. So, they ate as quickly as they could and buried any food left over to save for the future. Burying a meaty bone and leaving it in the earth for a while also softened the meat, making it easier to eat. The domesticated dogs of today have no need to bury, but retain the habit just the same.

Why do cats scratch furniture?

They do this to exercise their claws. Usually it is only cats which spend a lot of time indoors that do this. Cats that have plenty of freedom outdoors find trees or fences to scratch.

Why do cats always fall on their feet?

When a cat falls, it immediately turns its head to face the ground. Almost instantly the muscles of the body react, turning the rest of the body around so that the whole of the cat is in the correct position - feet first - before it reaches the ground.

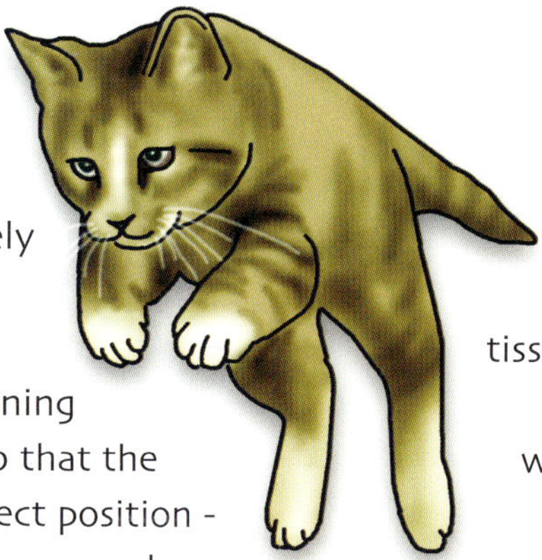

Why do cats have whiskers?

Cats' whiskers are embedded in a mass of tissue which contains many nerves. This makes the whiskers so sensitive that the cat can use them to measure the width of an opening, or to sense nearby objects when there is not enough light to see clearly.

Why are tigers striped?

A tiger's stripes act as a form of natural camouflage. One of the largest and most beautiful members of the cat family, the tiger is found mainly in Central and Southern Asia. Much of his area is jungle or grassy plain and the tiger's striped coat blends with the bamboos and slender grass that are found here, making the animal difficult to see. This is an important advantage when the tiger is hunting for prey.

What is catgut?

Catgut is a strong cord made from the intestines of sheep and other animals. It is used for stringing certain musical instruments and sports rackets. When sterilized, it is used as surgical thread.

Does catgut come from cats?

No. The 'cat' in 'catgut' is most likely derived from 'cattle' rather than 'cat'. Catgut is made from the intestines of sheep (and occasionally from horses, cattle and pigs).

Where can you find a cat without a tail?

The Isle of Man in the Irish Sea is the home of the tail-less Manx cat. Another breed of tail-less cat can be found in Japan and it is believed that the Manx breed originated in the Far East.

Is there anything else unusual about the Manx cat?

Yes. Its rear legs are longer than its front ones, thus giving it a curious hopping motion when it walks.

Why do cats purr?

Although cats seem to purr with pleasure, it is more likely that this noise is made to let others know of the cat's presence. A mother cat, for example, purrs to let her kittens know she is still around.

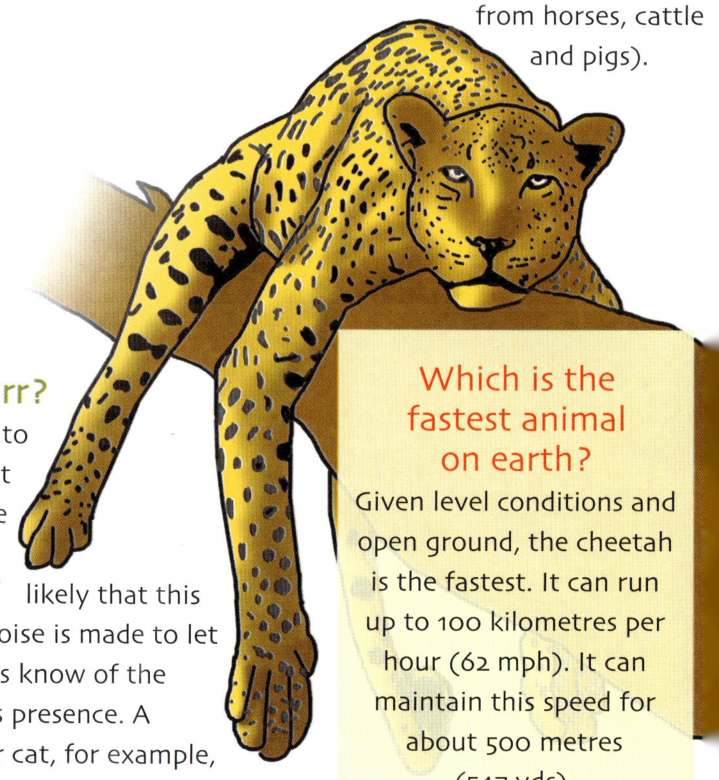

Which is the fastest animal on earth?

Given level conditions and open ground, the cheetah is the fastest. It can run up to 100 kilometres per hour (62 mph). It can maintain this speed for about 500 metres (547 yds).

What is the largest land mammal?

The African elephant. Adult males can weigh up to 8 tons and measure some 3-4 metres (10-13 ft) in height at the shoulder.

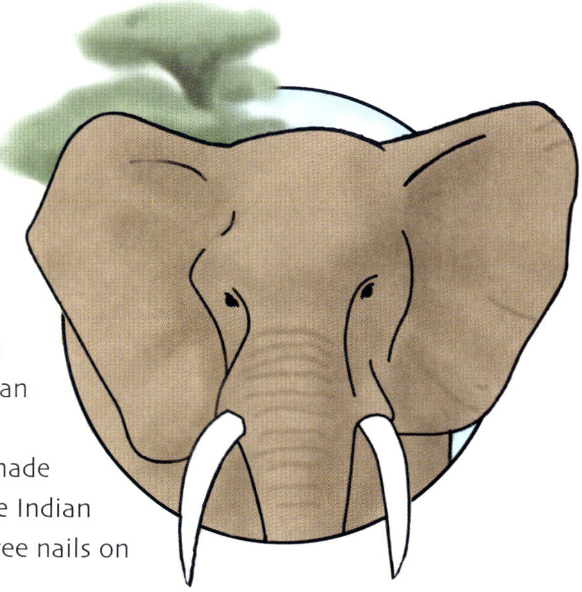

What is the difference between Indian and African elephants?

Although at first sight, the African and Indian elephants look alike, there are quite a few differences between them. For one, the African elephant has bigger ears than its Indian cousin. The head of the African elephant is more rounded and its eyes are larger. There are also differences in the trunks; that of an African elephant appears to be made up of segments and it has two small extensions at its tip, whereas the Indian has only one. The African elephant also has larger tusks, and only three nails on its hind feet, while the Indian elephant has four.

Which animal has the longest nose?

The African elephant, whose trunk measures 2.5 metres (8 ft 3 in).

Why are elephants often called Jumbo?

Jumbo was the name given to the first African elephant to appear at London Zoo in 1865. Many elephants since have been given the same name and, because he was an exceptionally big elephant the word 'jumbo' is often used to describe anything that is particularly large.

Which animal has the longest tail?

The Indian elephant - it has a tail of 1.5 metres (5 ft), not counting the tuft of hair at its end.

Why do birds eat grit?

As birds do not have teeth, they need some other means of breaking up their food, to prepare it for digestion. The grit eaten by some birds and the small bones consumed by birds of prey, goes into the gizzard with the food. Here, the muscular walls churn the grit or bones and food together. Softened by this action, the food continues on its way through the rest of their digestive system.

How fast can an ostrich run?

The ostrich is the fastest creature on two legs, so it can run pretty fast! It runs at usual speeds of 50 kilometres per hour (30 mph). But it can reach speeds of up to 70 kilometres per hour (43 mph) when escaping from predators.

Where do budgerigars come from?

A budgerigar is a species of Australian parakeet. The name 'budgerigar' comes from the Australian aborigine language and means 'good cockatoo'. In the wild, budgies are usually pale green with yellowish heads and brown bars on the wings. Breeding in captivity has developed other colours such as blue, white and mauve. The first pair were brought to England in 1840

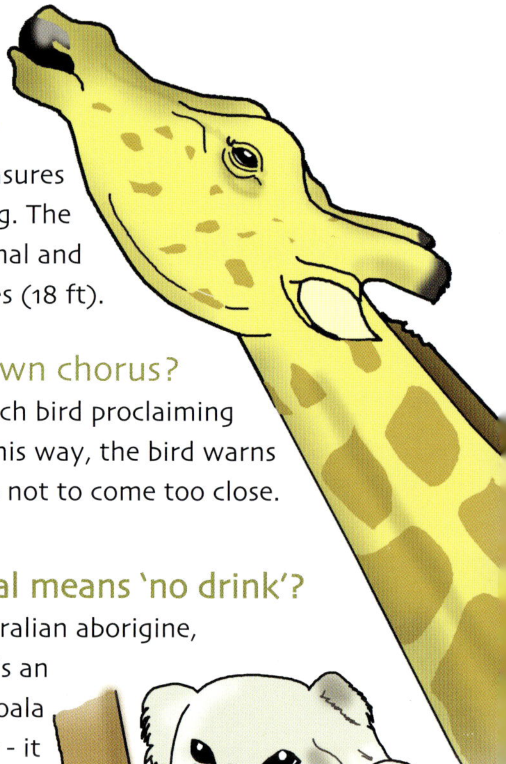

How long is a giraffe's neck?

On average a giraffe's neck measures about 2 metres (6 ft 5 in) long. The giraffe is the tallest land animal and can grow up to 5.5 metres (18 ft).

Why do birds sing a dawn chorus?

A dawn chorus is simply each bird proclaiming its right to its territory. In this way, the bird warns others of the same species not to come too close.

The name of which animal means 'no drink'?

In the language of the Australian aborigine, 'koala' means 'no drink'. It is an appropriate name as the koala seldom needs to drink water - it gets all the water it needs from eating eucalyptus leaves.

Where do bats go in the daytime?

Bats are nocturnal creatures - they come out at night. During the day they sleep, hanging upside down in some quiet dark place, like a barn or a cave.

What was the elephant bird?

The elephant bird (so called because of its size) lived in Madagascar in the Indian Ocean. A relative of the ostrich, it stood three metres (ten ft) tall and weighed up to 453 kilograms (1,000 lb). Its egg was 200 times bigger than a hen's egg. Madagascans would drill holes in the eggs and use them as water carriers - which held up to 14 litres (18 pints) of liquid! Sadly, the elephant bird is no longer alive - it became extinct over 300 years ago.

Why do woodpeckers peck?

Woodpeckers peck at trees to grab insects on the bark. They also peck to make a noise in the same way that other birds sing. And, of course, they peck to make a hole in a tree in which to build a nest.

What is a gecko?

The gecko is a small insect-eating lizard. It has a large head and a short, stocky body. Geckos are quite common in warm countries and they get their strange name from the clicking sound they make.

Which is the longest snake?

The Asiatic reticulated python is the longest snake in the world. It lives in southeast Asia and is over eight metres (26 ft) in length.

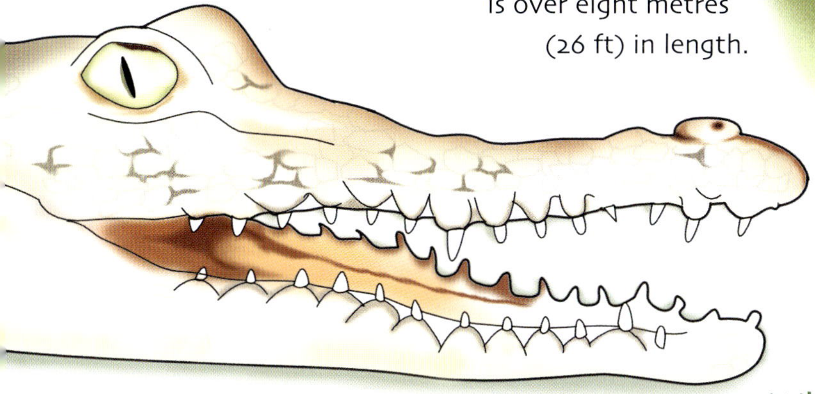

How strong is an alligator's jaw?

An alligator's jaw is actually quite weak. A man could easily hold an alligator's mouth shut - but it is not to be recommended!

Why do snakes stare?

Snakes appear to be staring simply because they do not have eyelids to cover their eyes as we do. This means that even when resting or hibernating, the snake's eyes are always open. Instead of eyelids snakes have a transparent membrane over the eyes to protect them.

Is it true that lizards squirt blood from their eyes?

Some members of the horned lizard family do squirt blood from their eyes as an unusual means of defence. The blood is thought to cause an irritation to the eyes of any enemy who gets too close.

How does a rattlesnake rattle?

The rattle sound is produced by a number of hollow rings fixed to the end of the snake's tail. The rings are made of a substance similar to that of our finger nails. They are joined loosely and rattle when the snake shakes its tail.

Are lizards poisonous?

Yes, but only two species: the gila monster and the Mexican bearded lizard. They are found in parts of Mexico and the USA.

Life Underwater

What are plankton?
Plankton are tiny life-forms that float in the sea in groups. The creatures are so small they are invisible to the naked eye, but they are a valuable and essential source of food for whales and other sea creatures.

How is coral formed?
Coral is made up of the skeletons of small creatures that live in the sea. The corals tend to live in large colonies, which build up over time to form coral reefs.

Where do eels come from?
This question puzzled biologists for centuries. An eel larva was first found in 1856 but Mondini, the Italian who discovered it, believed the creature was a type of fish. It was a man called Johannes Schmidt who discovered the breeding grounds of the European eel, in the Sargasso sea, south of Bermuda. The American eel breeds nearby.

How can you tell the difference between a dolphin and a porpoise?
The easiest way to tell the difference is to look at the head. Dolphins appear to have a beak, whereas the head of a porpoise is rounded.

Who was Pelorus Jack?
Pelorus Jack was the name of a porpoise which, from 1871 to 1912, guided ships through an area of dangerous sea near New Zealand. The waters had many dangerous currents and hidden rocks, but by following Jack the ships were able to navigate the channel safely. The porpoise was called Pelorus Jack as the ships sailed from Pelorus Sound.

What is a piranha?
The piranha is a fish that lives in the rivers of South America. It is particularly famous for its voraciousness. Four of the dozen or so species of piranha fish are dangerous. Pygocentrus piraya - the largest species - can reach lengths of up to 60 centimetres (2ft).

What is a manatee?
A manatee is an aquatic mammal of the sea-cow family. It is believed that these creatures inspired the legendary stories of mermaids.

How do fish breathe?
First, the fish takes water into its mouth. The water is forced over the gills inside the fish and out through the gill slits, which are usually on each side of the back part of the head. Blood vessels in the gills extract oxygen from the water and the blood then carries it around the body.

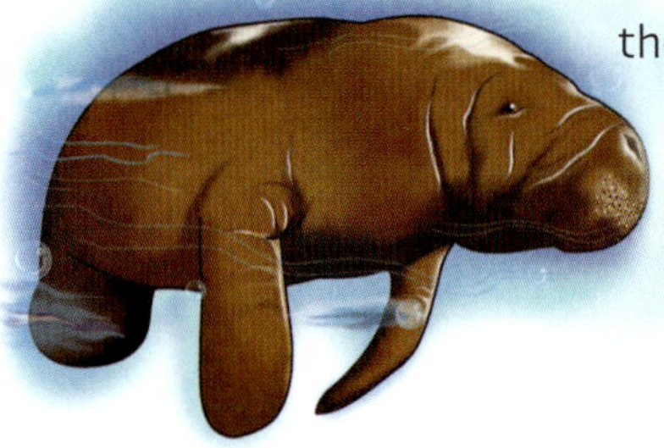

What is a seahorse?
Although it does not look like one, the seahorse is actually a fish. There are several different species of seahorse, found in warm seas in many parts of the world. They range in length from two centimetres (3/4 in) to 30 centimetres (11 3/4 in). Seahorses live among seaweed, hanging onto it with their tails. And as they are a similar colour to seaweed, seahorses are well camouflaged there.

Which is the biggest fish?
The whale shark. It lives in the warm parts of the Atlantic, Pacific and Indian Oceans and can measure up to 18 metres (59 ft) long and weigh 20,000 kg (44,092 lb).

Books

Who was Mrs Beeton?

Isabella Mayson was born in London in 1836. She married Samuel Beeton, a publisher, in 1856. Four years later she wrote her famous cookery book, Household Management.

What is the most famous cookery book?

It has to be Household Management by Isabella Beeton. Although first published in 1861, it contains numerous tips and recipes that are still used today.

Which is the world's oldest book?

Although several texts survive from before the birth of Christ, the earliest compiled book is probably the 'Codex Vaticanus' Bible, written in Greek around AD 350. It is preserved in the Vatican Museum, Rome.

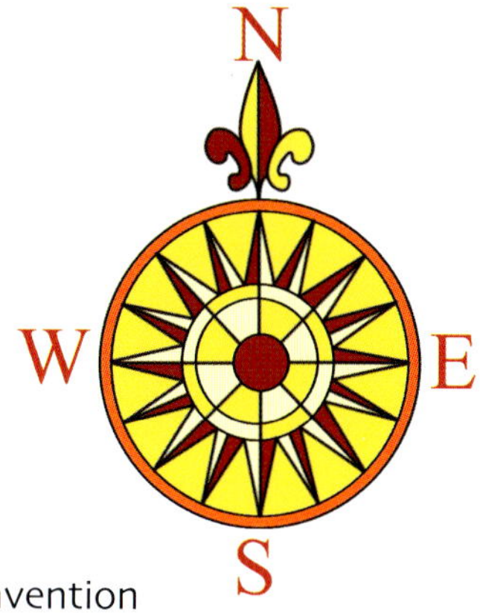

Which was the first printed book?

The earliest mechanically printed book is almost certainly the Gutenberg Bible, which was printed by Johann Gutenberg around 1455.

Why are maps drawn with north at the top?

Strictly speaking it doesn't matter which way up a map is drawn, provided the directions are indicated. Over many years, however, it has become standard practice to draw maps with north at the top. This convention probably dates back to about AD 160 when the Egyptian astronomer and scientist Claudius Ptolemy drew maps of the then known world. He placed north at the top and map-makers have followed suit ever since.

What is Burke's Peerage?

In 1826, John Burke published the first edition of a book listing all the nobles in Britain. Published every year since, it is entitled Genealogical and Heraldic History of the Peerage, Baronetage, and Knightage of the United Kingdom; it is popularly known as Burke's Peerage.

Who would use the Dewey Decimal System?

A librarian or someone using a library are the people most likely to use the Dewey Decimal System. The system is a method of classifying books so they can be easily sorted and found on the shelves. The main part of the system breaks down all knowledge into ten subject areas. Each area is then broken down further into ten sub-classes, which are broken down yet again into ten more sub-classes. Although it has been modified since its creation by Melvil Dewey in 1876, the Dewey System is still used in libraries today.

Who published the first dictionary?

The first known dictionary was published in 1502. It was produced in Italy by Ambrogio Calepino.

Who compiled the first encyclopedia?

In AD 77 the Roman scholar Pliny the Elder published the first known encyclopedia, Historia naturalis. It had 2,493 entries, for Pliny tried to cover all known knowledge.

Who were the Brontë sisters?

Charlotte, Emily and Anne Brontë were all 19th-century novelists. With their mother dead and their father a recluse, they would write stories together to pass the time. Eventually their ability to create fantasy was rewarded in the publication of their books, which today are among the classics of literature.

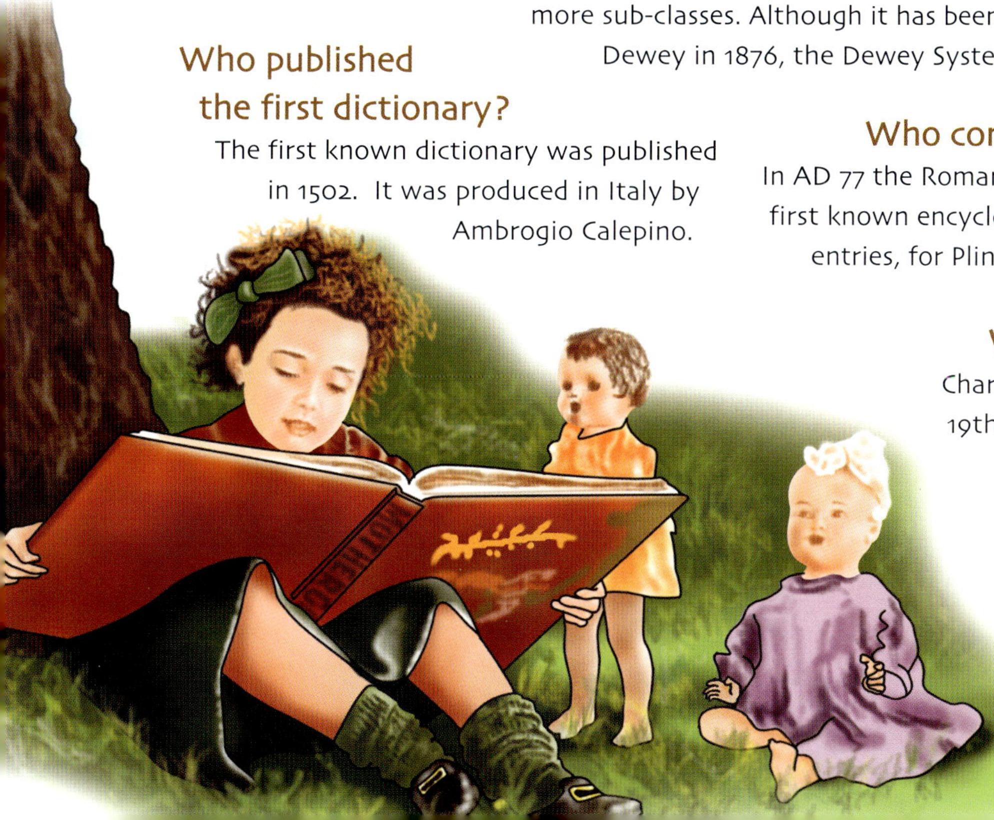

Making Music

How does one play an aeolian harp?

The aeolian harp is an oblong box over which strings of different thicknesses are stretched. It is a musical instrument, yet no-one plays it. To use an aeloian harp, it must be placed outside, where the wind can blow on it. The wind makes the strings vibrate to produce musical sounds. It gets its name from Aeolus, the Greek god of the winds.

What is a concerto?

A concerto is a piece of music composed for a solo instrument, accompanied by an orchestra. The purpose of a concerto is to highlight the expertise of the soloist.

What is a Stradivarius?

It is a violin. For almost 200 years the Amati family of Cremona, Italy, made superb violins. One of the family's apprentices was Antonio Stradivarius. Stradivarius violins were beautifully made and gave an excellent tone. As a result, they have become extremely valuable. Stradivarius is now regarded as the greatest violin maker of all time.

Who wrote the most concertos?

Antonio Vivaldi, who composed almost 500 known concertos (though some experts believe he wrote many more). Vivaldi also holds the record for the concerto with the most soloists. He wrote two concertos in which there are 11 soloist parts.

Who invented the clarinet?

The clarinet is a single-reed woodwind instrument. It was invented in its current form in about 1700, by Johann Christoph Denner. It has been popular with orchestras and jazz musicians since 1920.

Who invented the saxophone?

The saxophone was invented around 1840 by the Belgian craftsman Adolphe Sax. It was first played publicly in 1844 in Paris, where Sax had a workshop. It is said the instrument was held together with string and sealing wax.

What is a Cor Anglais?

Cor Anglais is another name for the English horn, which is a reed instrument of the oboe family.

What is a plectrum?

If you watch guitarists, you will see they are often plucking the strings with a plectrum - a small piece of bone or plastic. Plectrums prevent the fingers from becoming sore.

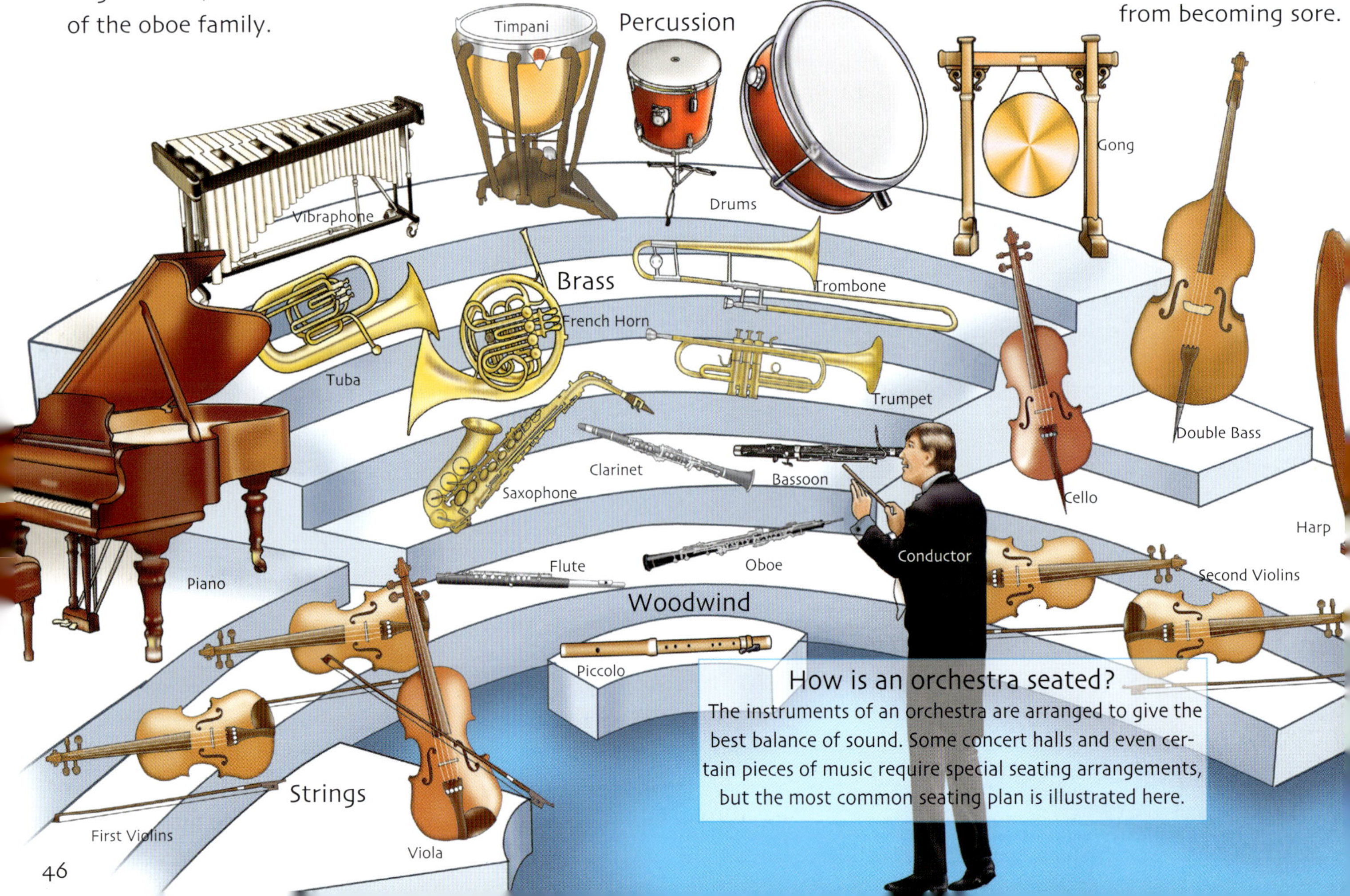

How is an orchestra seated?

The instruments of an orchestra are arranged to give the best balance of sound. Some concert halls and even certain pieces of music require special seating arrangements, but the most common seating plan is illustrated here.

Games and Sports

Who was the first person to swim the English Channel?

Matthew Webb entered the water at Dover at 12.56 pm on 24th May 1875. Next day, he stepped ashore at Cap Gris-Nez, France, becoming the first person to swim the English Channel without a life jacket. It took him 21 hours 45 minutes and it is thought that he actually swam a distance of 61 kilometres (38 miles) to make the 33 km (21 miles) crossing because tides pushed him off course.

How old is chess?

Chess is an ancient game. The name 'chess' comes from the Persian word 'shah' (meaning king or ruler) and old Persian and Indian writings show the game was known in these countries as early as the 6th century.

How was rugby invented?

During a football match at Rugby School in 1823, a pupil, William Webb Ellis, picked up the ball and ran with it. The idea caught on and the game was soon played at other schools. The Rugby Football Union was founded on January 26th 1871.

When was football first played?

Ball games similar to football can be traced back to ancient China, Greece and Rome, but the origins of the modern game stem from England. The original game was a disorganised rough-and-tumble and it was not until 1846 that the first deliberate rules were formulated. The modern game, however, was formally established with the formation of the Football Association in 1863.

Who invented snooker?

Credit for the game's invention is given to a British Army colonel, Sir Neville Chamberlain, who in 1875 first played the game at his club in India.

What is the Calcutta Cup?

It is an award given to the winner of the annual Rugby Union game between England and Scotland. It is so called because the cup was made from rupees left in the bank by the Calcutta Rugby Club (which was disbanded in 1878).

How did the Derby get its name?

In 1779, Sir Charles Bunbury and Lord Derby tossed a coin to decide the name of a race to be held at Epsom for the first time the following year. If it hadn't been for the fact that Lord Derby won the toss, the race could now be known as the Bunbury.

When was the first Oxford-Cambridge boat race?

The boat race between Oxford University and Cambridge University is an annual event. The first race took place in 1829 at Henley-on-Thames.

How did the Oaks horse race get its name?

The Oaks, run annually at Epsom, received its name from Lambert's Oaks, a cluster of trees near the racecourse. The race was first run in 1779.

Who was the first woman to swim the English Channel?

Gertrude Ederle on 6th August 1926. She swam from Cap Gris-Nez in France to Deal in England in 14 hours 39 minutes.

When were jigsaw puzzles invented?

John Spilsbury, a teacher at Harrow school in the 1760s, was searching for a new way to teach his pupils geography. One day he cut up a map of the British Isles and asked his class to reassemble it. The idea proved successful, and soon 'dissected puzzles' became a fashionable tool for teaching geography, history and religion. These first puzzles did not interlock, and were produced for educational purposes only. Interlocking puzzles were developed in the 20th century.

When was overarm bowling first used in cricket?

In the early days of cricket, it was the custom for bowlers to bowl underarm. Now overarm bowling is the norm. The person responsible for this change was John Willes of Kent, but it seems that the real credit should go to his sister, Christine. Christine used to bowl for John at their home to give him batting practice, but the fullness of her skirt made it impossible for her to bowl underarm. John found the round-arm style she developed more difficult to parry. He adopted the same style but umpires accused him of throwing. In spite of frequent 'no ball' decisions and spectators rushing onto pitches in protest, he persevered with his new delivery. But in 1822, when Kent played the MCC at Lords, a 'no ball' call proved just too much. Willes stormed off the field, mounted his horse, and rode out of the cricket ground for good. Thirteen years later the rules were changed and overarm bowling received official blessing.

Who invented Monopoly?

Charles Darrow, a heating engineer of Philadelphia, USA, devised the game of Monopoly between 1931 and 1933. He offered it to the USA's foremost games manufacturer, but they turned it down because it was too complicated. Darrow then decided to print some boards himself. The game became quite popular and Parker Brothers changed their mind. They first sold it nationally at Christmas 1935 and it remains popular all over the world to this day.

How wide is a cricket bat?

In 1776, Mr White of Surrey played cricket with a bat so large it obscured the wicket. Two days later the Hambledon Club, then the ruling body of English cricket, decreed that cricket bats be no more than 10.8 centimetres (4.25 in) wide, a rule that still applies today.

Was cricket ever banned?

Yes, during the reign of Henry VIII. Anyone caught playing cricket on the King's land was fined £20 and sent to prison for up to three years.

Has anyone ever scored 6 runs off 6 balls in cricket?

Sir Garfield Sobers achieved this amazing feat at Swansea in 1968. The ball with which he made this record score is now on display in the museum at Nottingham cricket ground.

What has been the most unusual reason for stopping a cricket match?

One of the most unusual reasons must have been during a match in South Africa: there was an urgent telephone call for one of the players - his wife wanted to know where he had put the soap!

Which horse race was named after a Tsar?

The Cesarewitch, first run in 1839, was named after the Tsarevitch (or Cesarewitch) Alexander, later Alexander II, who was in England at the time.

Where was the first ever World Cup held?

Uruguay in 1930. Uruguay beat Argentina 4-2.

What is the Calgary Stampede?

This is an annual rodeo (a sort of tournament for cowboys) held in Calgary, Canada.

When was the Grand National first run?

The Grand National was first run in 1837. This famous steeplechase covers a distance of some seven kilometres (four miles) and is held annually at Liverpool's Aintree Racecourse.

What is a boomerang?

It is a curved, flat piece of wood best known as a weapon of the Australian aborigine. There are two types of boomerangs, the war boomerang (which does not return to the thrower) and the sporting boomerang (which does come back if it has not hit anything). Sporting boomerangs can be anything up to half a metre in length but the war boomerang is twice as long and usually requires both hands to throw it.

Which swords are used in the sport of fencing?

There are three weapons used in modern fencing: the foil, the épée and the sabre. The foil has a long thin blade with a button on its tip, the épée is stiffer and heavier than the foil and the sabre has a flat blade.

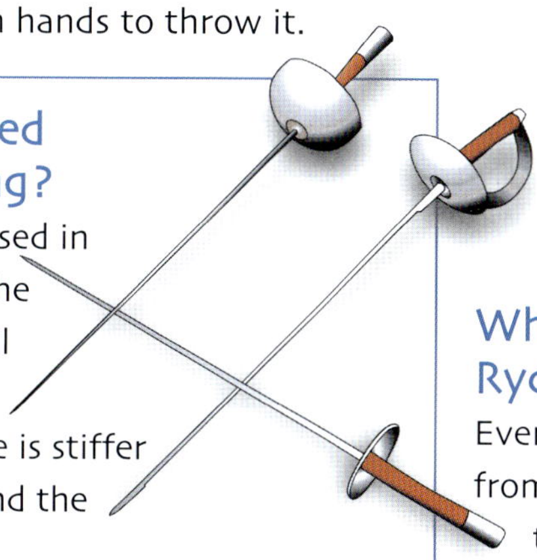

What is the Ryder Cup?

Every two years, professional male golfers from Britain and Ireland play a team from the USA. The winning team is given the Ryder Cup, which was first awarded by Samuel Ryder in 1927.

Has anyone ever disputed a cricket umpire's decision?

This happens on occasion, but the most dramatic case occurred during a match between teams from Kent and Essex in 1776. The match ended in a gunfight and three players were shot dead!

Who invented the crossword puzzle?

It was Arthur Wynne in 1913. A newspaper editor, he was searching for something 'fun' for his paper New York World. The first crossword puzzle was published on 21 December and became an instant success.

Fascinating Facts

What is batik?

Batik is an Indonesian technique of dying fabric. Wax is applied to areas that are not to be dyed and then the material is placed in a cool dye. To remove the wax, the material is then set in hot water. This action can be repeated several times with different colours and patterns.

Why do some trousers have turn-ups?

King Edward VII was one of the first men to wear turn-ups. It's not known who invented the style but according to tradition, there is a story of an Englishman who was invited to a party in New York. He turned up his trouser legs because it was raining. When he arrived at the party everyone thought this was a new English fashion and the idea caught on.

What is a kimono?

A traditional Japanese costume consisting of a single piece of silk which is held around the waist by a sash.

Where is the Bermuda Triangle?

The Bermuda Triangle covers a vast area of the Atlantic Ocean between Bermuda, Puerto Rico and Miami. Many strange stories have been told of the mysterious disappearances of ships and aeroplanes in this area. But similar tales are told of other parts of the world, and usually improve with each telling. It is impossible to say for certain how much of the Bermuda Triangle mystery is fact and how much is fiction.

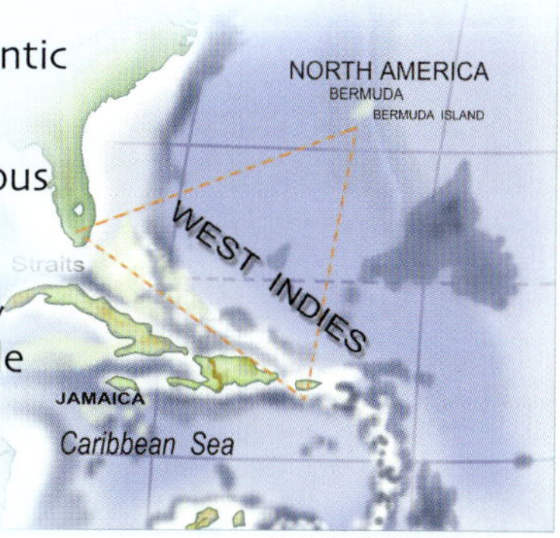

What is Morse Code?

Morse code is a method of sending messages by a series of long and short signals. The signals are sent using a telegraph or by flashes with a torch. In written form, dots represent short signals, dashes long ones.

Did Sir Walter Raleigh lay down his cloak for the Queen?

According to tradition, Raleigh laid his cloak over a puddle so that Queen Elizabeth I could walk on it and not get her feet wet. Although a nice story, it is an unlikely one. It was probably made up by the British historian Thomas Fuller, who liked to put interesting tales in his writing to pep up any dull parts!

Is it possible to be afraid of a messy room?

Yes, a person who has an irrational fear of untidiness is said to be suffering from ataxiophobia.

Why is there a best man at weddings?

Being best man at a wedding is an honour few men would welcome, if they realised what they're supposed to be best at. The answer is fighting! In days gone by it was the best man's job to defend the bride and groom should anyone try to take the girl away. The best man had to do the fighting because the groom had other matters on his mind!

What is the Blarney Stone?

It is a stone high up in the battlements of Blarney Castle in Ireland. Kissing the stone is said to give one eloquence. But the stone is on the outside wall and one has to lean over with someone holding onto one's legs to reach it!

When was tartan banned?

It was against the law to wear tartan dress in Scotland following the Scottish Rebellion of 1745. The ban remained in force until the law was abolished in 1782.

What happened to Sir Walter Raleigh's head after his execution?

Legend has it that after Raleigh's execution in 1618, his wife kept his head. She carried it around with her in a bag for 29 years, until her own death.

What is glass made of?

Glass is made by fusing sand with soda ash and lime or with lead oxide. It is thought the ancient Egyptians were the first people to make glass.

How is glass produced?

The three basic ingredients are mixed with cullet (broken glass), dolomite and saltcake and are then melted down in a furnace. The intense heat causes the substances to fuse into one molten mass, which flows out of the furnace into a float chamber. Here, the glass floats on a bed of molten tin. The glass is cooled slightly and then passed over water-cooled pipes. Further cooling is achieved by passing the glass under a series of water sprays which also helps to strengthen it. When the glass has cooled completely, it is cut to size.

What is topiary?

Topiary is the art of clipping hedges and bushes into ornamental shapes. A new plant is usually trained to grow around a wire shape and is clipped regularly to maintain that shape.

Is the Willow Pattern Chinese?

No, the pattern was designed by an English potter, Thomas Turner, in about 1780. After it became popular in England, the pattern was copied by Chinese potters to sell their wares to the British.

Is there a story in the Willow Pattern?

The Willow Pattern is said to tell the story of a Chinese girl who ran off with her father's secretary. The father pursued the couple but they were then transformed into doves so they could escape him.

Why are typewriter keys arranged in a certain order?

At first sight, it would appear that a typewriter keyboard is laid out in a nonsensical way. The top line of keys, for instance, are QWERTYUIOP. There is a reason for this odd arrangement. When Christopher Latham Sholes and his colleagues invented the first practical typewriter in 1873, they had quite a problem with the typebars clashing together. To overcome this, they arranged the keys so that the most used letters in the English language were positioned well apart. This design proved so successful that much the same layout is used to this day.

What is an arctophile?

Someone who collects teddy bears!

Who invented the typewriter?

Henry Mills, an English engineer, was awarded a patent in 1714 for a machine that impressed letters on paper. Over the next 150 years, many other writing machines were invented, some more successful than others, but it was not until 1873 that the forerunner of the modern typewriter was introduced. Christopher Latham Sholes, Carlos Glidden and Samuel Soule persuaded the Remington company to produce their design, which came onto the market a year later.

What was the earliest form of shorthand?

A system created by Marcus Tiro in 63 BC. He used his shorthand to record the speeches of Cicero, a Roman statesman.

What is touch-typing?

Touch-typing is the skill of using a type-writer without looking at the keys. The touch-typist uses all the fingers of both hands in the most efficient manner possible.

What is the indian 'rope trick'?

It is a magic trick in which a long rope is made rigid and a boy climbs up it to the top. When he reaches the top, he disappears. Magicians, however, believe it is merely a traveller's tale.

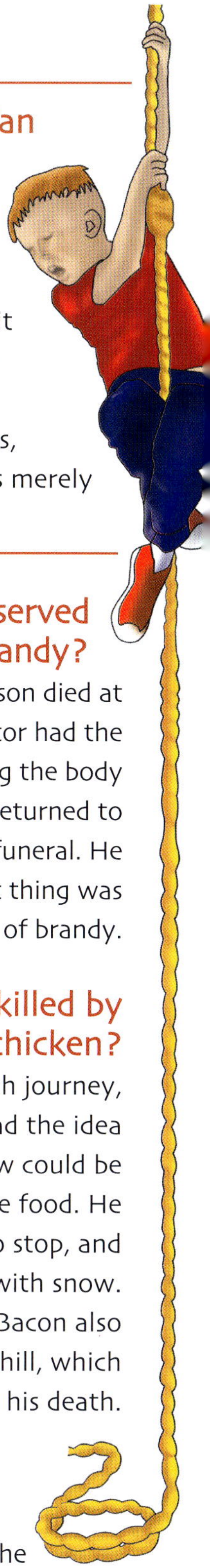

Who was preserved in brandy?

When Admiral Nelson died at sea in 1805, the doctor had the problem of preserving the body so it could be returned to England for a hero's funeral. He decided that the best thing was to put it in a barrel of brandy.

Who was killed by a frozen chicken?

During a stagecoach journey, Francis Bacon had the idea that ice and snow could be used to preserve food. He asked the driver to stop, and stuffed a chicken with snow. Unfortunately, Bacon also caught a chill, which resulted in his death.

What was a press gang?

For centuries, the threat of brutal, enforced military service hung over able-bodied men between the ages of 18 and 25. The service was known as impressment, and the bands of ruffians who carried out the recruit-ment were called press gangs. They would snatch unwary men and con-demn them to service under the harsh conditions of naval ships.

Who was Uncle Sam?

The name 'Uncle Sam' is often used as a nickname for the USA. The term first came into use in New York around 1812. It is said that a butcher, Samuel Wilson, known as Uncle Sam, supplied beef to the US Army. As the meat crates had US (for United States) stamped on them, the meat became known as Uncle Sam's meat. It was not long before the name Uncle Sam was used for the USA tself.

What is a cockney?

Sometimes, the word 'cockney' is used to describe any person from London. This, however, is not correct. To be a true cockney, the person has to be born within the sound of Bow Bells (the bells of the church of St Mary-Le-Bow in Cheapside). The term 'cockney' is also used to describe the speech and accent of people born in this area.

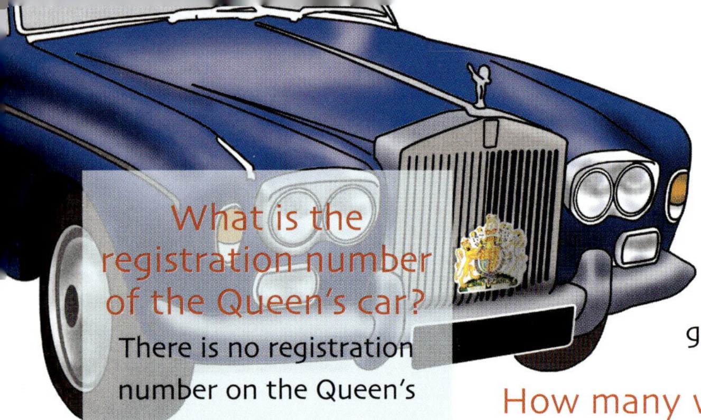

What is the registration number of the Queen's car?

There is no registration number on the Queen's car. Her Majesty's cars are the only ones in Britain that do not require registration plates.

What is the Lutine Bell?

The Lutine Bell came from the wreck of HMS Lutine, which sank during a storm off the Dutch coast in 1799. The bell was recovered in 1859 and now hangs in the insurance house Lloyds of London. It is rung when important news is to be announced - one ring means good news and two rings means bad news.

Who owns Ayers Rock?

The Australian government transferred ownership of Ayers Rock to the Aboriginal people in 1985. The Australian Aborigines regard Ayers Rock as a sacred place and there are many ancient rock paintings in the numerous caves around its base. The enormous rock is incorporated in the Uluru National Park, Central Australia.

Which British king was crowned on Christmas Day?

William of Normandy, better known as William the Conqueror, in 1066.

Which member of the British royal family was born on Christmas Day?

HRH Princess Alexandra was born on 25th December 1936.

What was the King's evil?

It was the nickname given to a disease called scrofula. Many believed it could be cured by a touch from the sovereign.

How many words are there in the English language?

There are over 600,000 words in the English language, but even the most clever people only know about 20,000. On average, some 2,000 words are used in everyday speech.

Which country has the oldest flag?

The world's oldest national flag is that of Denmark. It has remained unchanged, with a white cross on a red background, since 1219.

What is the world's most widely spoken language?

Mandarin Chinese. The second most widely spoken language is English.

How old is the Bank of England?

In 1694, Scottish financier William Paterson suggested a 'Bank of England' be set up in order to lend £1,200,000 to the government. King William III approved the idea on 27th July 1694. It was planned that the bank would close down after a decade, but the Bank of England is now over 300 years old.

What is the Old Lady of Threadneedle Street?

The Old Lady of Threadneedle Street is a nickname for the Bank of England in Threadneedle Street, London. In 1797, the artist James Gillray depicted the bank as an elderly lady wearing a dress of £1 notes, seated on a chest marked 'Bank of England'.

How is lead put into a pencil?

The first stage in the manufacture of pencils consists of making a wooden slat - a flat piece of wood. Several parallel grooves are then cut into each slat. It is into these grooves that the leads (strips of soft graphite) are laid. A second grooved slat is then placed on top of the first, and the two are glued together with the leads in between. The slats are moulded into the shape of pencils before the individual pencils are separated and passed on to the finishing process.

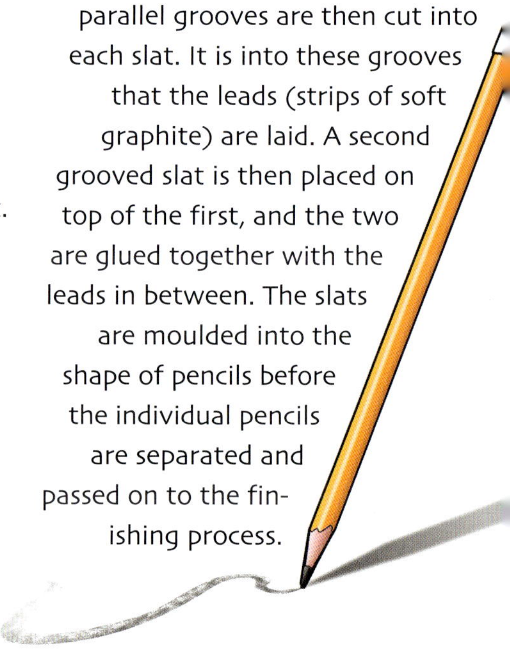

Who composed the song 'Happy Birthday'?

In 1892, Patty Smith Hill and Mildred Hill wrote the song 'Good Morning to You' for pupils at their school in Louisville, Kentucky, USA. Although their tune is now sung with the words 'Happy Birthday to You', this version has been popular only since its publication in 1935. It has been sung all over the world since, and even in space - on 8th March 1969 it was sung by the Apollo IX astronauts.

What is the Stone of Scone?

The Stone of Scone is a large piece of sandstone kept at Westminster Abbey in London. It was used in the coronation ceremony for Scottish kings until 1296, when King Edward I took it to England as a war trophy. In 1328, it was agreed that the stone should be returned to Scotland - an agreement that has yet to be fulfilled.

Who stole the Stone of Scone?

Amazingly, the 204 kilogram (450 lb) stone was once stolen from Westminster Abbey! On Christmas Day 1950, four students removed the stone. Months later, it was found at the ruined Abbey of Arbroath, Scotland and police returned it to London. Outside a hotel in Scotland is a replica of the stone but some people believe this is the original and that the one now in Westminster Abbey is the replica!

How old is Buckingham Palace?

Buckingham Palace has been the London residence of British royalty since 1830. The present building stands on the site of Buckingham House, which was built in 1703 for the Duke of Buckingham. King George III bought it for his wife, Queen Charlotte, in 1762 and for the next 50 years it was known as the Queen's House. Work began on the present building in 1825.

Why are waste pipes U-shaped?

Waste pipes from toilets and sinks are shaped like a letter U or a letter S to trap water in them. This acts as a seal that prevents foul air from the drains getting into the house.

Why is the piggy bank so called?

Although many piggy banks are shaped like pigs, this is not the reason for their name. The name comes from a ceramic material called 'pygg', which was once used for making ornaments. As the coin saver was made from pygg, it seemed obvious to make it in the shape of a pig.

Why are clowns often called Joey?

Clowns are often called Joey in honour of Joseph Grimaldi, who lived from 1779 to 1837. Grimaldi was a brilliant clown, singer, dancer and actor and is regarded as one of the greatest clowns of all time.

Does Timbuktu really exist?

Yes, it is a town in West Africa. For many years, it was an important market town and a centre for caravan routes.

What is the Magic Circle?

The Magic Circle is a club for magicians. There are lots of magic clubs around the world where magicians meet to discuss the latest tricks, but the Magic Circle in London is the most famous.

Why do we use & for 'and'?

The symbol & (an ampersand) comes from the Latin word 'et' (which means 'and'). The ampersand is simply the 'e' and 't' of et put together. Ampersands are used in hundreds of languages around the world.

Who put up the famous Hollywood sign?

In 1923, M H Sherman was selling homes in Los Angeles. To publicise the houses, he had a large billboard erected on Lee Mountain with the name of the estate, HOLLYWOODLAND. In 1944, the estate company moved from the area and passed 182 hectares (450 acres) of land, including the sign, to the Los Angeles Parks Department. Five years later, it was rebuilt but the 'land' was removed from it. In 1973, a new sign was built, and was unveiled on 14th November 1978.